Eustace Rogers Conder

Outlines of the life of Christ:

A guide to the study of the chronology, harmony, and purpose of the Gospels

Eustace Rogers Conder

Outlines of the life of Christ:
A guide to the study of the chronology, harmony, and purpose of the Gospels

ISBN/EAN: 9783337714543

Printed in Europe, USA, Canada, Australia, Japan

Cover: Foto ©ninafisch / pixelio.de

More available books at **www.hansebooks.com**

THE R. T. S. LIBRARY—ILLUSTRATED

OUTLINES

OF THE

LIFE OF CHRIST

A Guide to the Study

OF THE

CHRONOLOGY, HARMONY, AND PURPOSE
OF THE GOSPELS

BY

EUSTACE R. CONDER, M.A., D.D.

AUTHOR OF 'THE BASIS OF FAITH,' ETC.

"Other foundation can no man lay than that is laid, which is Jesus Christ."—1 CORINTHIANS iii. 11

WITH FOUR ILLUSTRATIONS

THE RELIGIOUS TRACT SOCIETY
56, PATERNOSTER ROW; 65, ST. PAUL'S CHURCHYARD
AND 164, PICCADILLY
1887

LONDON:
PRINTED BY WILLIAM CLOWES AND SONS, LIMITED,
STAMFORD STREET AND CHARING CROSS.

EDITOR'S PREFACE.

This book is included in the R. T. S. Library in the hope that a clear and scholarly outline of the Life of the Saviour, by such a competent writer as Dr. Conder, will prove a boon to many who cannot afford to buy expensive works. Sunday School Teachers especially will find here very much to help them in their study of the Gospels. In a small space they get the results of the latest and best scholarship on the most important of all subjects.

AUTHOR'S PREFACE.

The present volume does not enter into any rivalry with those large and learned works on "the Life of Christ" which have issued from the press of late years in rapid succession, and whose large circulation bears witness to the undying interest of this inexhaustible theme. It aims at meeting a widely-felt want, by presenting in the most condensed form consistent with practical utility and interest, a trustworthy guide to the study of the chronology of the Gospel history, and of the harmony, contents, and purpose of the Four Gospels. It is therefore neither a compendium of the literature of the Gospels, nor a manual of controversy concerning the Gospels, but simply an aid to the study of the Gospels.

Those who wish to acquaint themselves with the opinions of eminent scholars on controverted points in the Gospel narrative (and what point has not been controverted?) will find abundant store of quotations and references in the learned and popular works of Dr. Farrar and Dr. Geikie; in McClellan's very learned and able work, *The Four Gospels;* and (in the most compact and convenient form) in Andrews's *Bible Student's Life of Our Lord.* With reference to sceptical criticism, Ebrard's *Gospel History* (Clark's translation) may be consulted with advantage. It is superfluous here to remind the student of other works in which the same ground is traversed, with diverse degrees of accuracy, knowledge, and clearness:— commentaries, Bible dictionaries, and works on New Testament Introduction.

The aim of the present Writer has been to place the instructed and thoughtful English reader, as far as possible, in a position to judge for himself on the questions which meet us in the study of the Gospels. For this purpose it is of first importance to draw a sharp line between facts in evidence and conjectures; between the authority of *testimony* and the authority of *opinion;* and to understand clearly, that the opinions and conjectures of even the most learned scholars do not constitute evidence. The placid dogmatism of contented ignorance is scarcely more to be dreaded than the superficial mimicry of scholarship which consists in knowing the names of a number of eminent writers who support a certain view, and of a number of others equally eminent who oppose it. To weigh authorities against one another, you need a capacious and delicate balance. But in not a few even of the most important questions, it is really an easier task for a well-taught, candid, clear-headed reader to form his own judgment with well-grounded confidence, than to decide on which side authority preponderates. Even in questions of translation, where the most accomplished scholar has no right to give a positive verdict (as in the question whether to translate, in Matt. vi. 13, "from evil," or "from the evil one"), the English reader may be quite competent to form his own opinion from the context and the sense.

It is of scarcely less importance to perceive clearly at what point evidence stops short, and conjecture and opinion form our only light. An overstrained effort after an unattainable degree of certainty and accuracy is apt to beget a reaction towards doubt and confusion. In the following pages, accordingly, some of the most intricate problems on which harmonists have exercised their ingenuity are set aside, on the simple principle that the "order" which St. Luke leads us to expect in his Gospel (chap. i. 1) is by no means necessarily always the order of time; order of topic being no less important and natural; and that it is therefore a vain labour to attempt to give to every incident or saying its exact chronological place.

The main order of events and dates, apart from these subordinate details, will be found closely to correspond with that adopted by the learned and judicious Dr. Robinson. As this is in no sense a following of his lead, but results from careful independent examination of every date and authority, this agreement may safely be accepted as no unimportant confirmation of the results here sought to be established.

Some points, especially in the earlier portion of the Gospel history, might perhaps with advantage have received fuller treatment. This defect, if such it be, has arisen from anxiety to keep the volume within very moderate limit as to size. If the outline is correctly and clearly drawn, the reader will find little difficulty in filling in any omitted details.

If thoughtful and devout readers of the Gospels find in these pages as much profit and interest as the composition of them has afforded the Writer, they will not be sent forth in vain; with which hope and prayer he humbly commends them to the blessing of God.

TABLE OF CONTENTS.

PART I.
INTRODUCTION.

SECTION I.
PAGE
DATE OF THE NATIVITY 11

SECTION II.
THE FULNESS OF TIME 22

PART II.
THE THIRTY YEARS.

SECTION I.
INFANCY 30

SECTION II.
LIFE AT NAZARETH 35

SECTION III.
THE EVE OF THE MINISTRY 44

PART III.
THE MINISTRY.

SECTION I.
FIRST YEAR, A.D. 27–28 54

SECTION II.
SECOND YEAR, A.D. 28–29 76

SECTION III.
THIRD YEAR, A.D. 29–30 101

PART IV.
CONCLUSION OF THE GOSPEL HISTORY.

SECTION I.
THE SUFFERINGS OF CHRIST 130

SECTION II.
THE RESURRECTION 161

SECTION III.
FROM EASTER TO PENTECOST 176

INDEX OF TEXTS 187

LIST OF ILLUSTRATIONS.

THE SEA OF GALILEE ... ... *Frontispiece*
NAZARETH 36
THE SOWER 90
JERUSALEM 160

OUTLINES
OF THE
LIFE OF CHRIST.

PART I.
INTRODUCTION.

SECTION I.
DATE OF THE NATIVITY.

THE PLACE of our Saviour's birth is by two of the Evangelists (Matthew and Luke) declared to have been "Bethlehem of Judæa." The TIME was "in the days of Herod, the King of Judæa;" and from St. Matthew's account we may gather that it was not long before Herod's death. Each Gospel presents a view of the facts accordant with its own special character and purpose. St. Matthew shows us the fulfilment of Old Testament prophecy in the birth at Bethlehem of Him who was born King of the Jews. St. Luke exhibits the secret working of God's world-wide providence, employing the heathen power of imperial Rome in so ordering events, that unto all nations should be born, "in the city of David, a Saviour who is Christ the Lord."

In order to determine the date of the Nativity with such accuracy as may be found possible, therefore, we have first to ascertain the date of Herod's death, and then to consider by what interval of time our Saviour's birth probably preceded it. Neither of these points is free from difficulty. Absolute certainty (let us at once candidly admit) is not attainable. But when the facts are clearly stated, they lead to a conclusion in which we may rest with a near approach to certainty, which is greatly confirmed when we find how the date thus determined harmonizes with all the after facts of the Gospel history.

Herod the Great reigned, as Josephus informs us (*Ant.* xvii. 8), thirty-four years from the time when he took Jerusalem by storm, and put Antigonus to death. This was in the month Sivan, in the summer of A.U.C. 717 (B.C. 37), three years after Herod had been made king by the Roman Senate (*Ant.* xiv. chaps. 14 and 16). According to our mode of reckoning, therefore, Herod's thirty-fourth year would be from Sivan of the year 750 (B.C. 4) to Sivan of 751 (B.C. 3). But the Jewish custom was to reckon regnal years from the beginning of the Jewish sacred year, at whatever time the actual accession might take place. Consequently Herod's thirty-fourth year, by Jewish reckoning, was from 1 Nisan 750 to the eve of 1 Nisan 751 (B.C. 4-3). Between these two dates his death must have occurred. And even if he died in the first week of Nisan he would be held to have "reigned thirty-four years," that is, entered his thirty-fourth year as king, though the actual anniversary of his accession was not till between two or three months later.

Now, if the account given by Josephus be carefully studied (*Ant.* xvii. 6-11 ; *Wars*, i. 33 ; ii. 1, 2), it will be found to furnish decisive proof that the death of Herod occurred shortly before the Passover. The facts may be briefly stated thus. Herod died at

DATE OF THE NATIVITY

Jericho, having previously gone to the hot baths of Callirhoë, beyond Jordan, in the vain hope of gaining some alleviation of his intolerable sufferings. Archelaus, his son and successor, after providing a magnificent funeral, and observing the necessary week of mourning, came to Jerusalem, sacrificed in the Temple, and addressed the people in regal state. At first he was well received, but in the evening a public lamentation burst forth throughout the city, not for King Herod, but for certain Rabbins whom he had cruelly put to death. These Rabbins, when the king was thought to be dying, had instigated their disciples to hew down a golden eagle, erected by him over the great gate of the Temple. Herod had taken savage vengeance, causing the Rabbins and their most active followers to be burnt alive. The Passover, Josephus tells us, was now approaching (*Wars*, ii. 1: 3; *Ant.* xvii. 9: 3). The multitudes who on that account were arriving in Jerusalem swelled the disturbance to a formidable sedition, which Archelaus suppressed with severity worthy of his father, three thousand persons being massacred by his troops. After establishing order in this fashion he hastened to Rome, to seek the imperial sanction to his father's testament, appointing him King of Judæa. At Cæsarea he met the Procurator of Syria, on his way to Jerusalem, to take charge of Herod's wealth in the name of the Roman government. No exact dates are given by Josephus, but Archelaus was at Rome before Pentecost (*Wars*, ii. 3 : 1);—manifestly in the summer of the same year.

The question then arises: Was the Passover which thus followed the death of Herod that of B.C. 4, or B.C. 3? Here we have a remarkable note of time. On the night after the Rabbins were burned, an eclipse of the moon took place (*Ant.* xvii. 6: 4). Astronomers find that the only eclipse to which this statement can refer occurred on March 13, B.C. 4

14   OUTLINES OF THE LIFE OF CHRIST.

(A.U.C. 750). The succeeding full moon, April 11, was that of the Passover (Nisan 14–15); and Nisan 1 fell on March 29. Now, if we deduct the seven days of mourning, including the funeral, together with at least three or four days for the visit of Archelaus to Jerusalem and the influx of the multitude before the Passover, we are thrown back to April 1 or March 31 (Nisan 4 or 3), as the latest day on which we can suppose the death of Herod to have happened. A new difficulty, therefore, here meets us. Can the events related by Josephus as having happened between the burning of the Rabbins and the death of Herod be supposed to have occurred within the short space of eighteen or nineteen days? The reply is, first, that nothing is related by Josephus which might not really have occurred in less than three weeks; and, secondly, that far greater difficulties oppose the supposition that a year intervened between the martyrdom of the Rabbins and the death of the Tyrant. The violent popular lamentation, quickly swelling into riot and insurrection, proves the event to have been recent. It was the fact of Herod being believed to be at the point of death, which encouraged the Rabbins and their adherents to that rash exploit for which they paid so dear. Immediately afterwards, Herod's disease (or, rather, complication of diseases) became frightfully aggravated; and his sufferings were so intense, and of so dreadful a nature, that it is impossible to suppose a man of seventy, who had lived a profligate life, lingering on such a death-bed for a whole year. And if the events of the closing three weeks or fortnight of his life were crowded together with surprising rapidity, like the rush of waters hurrying to the brink of the precipice, yet the attempt to stretch them over twelve months is inconsistent with the history, and would leave the last year of his reign almost a blank.

All these considerations therefore compel us to

place the death of Herod in the Spring of A.U.C. 750 = B.C. 4.

This conclusion is in exact harmony with the statement of Josephus (*Ant.* xviii. 4: 6), that Philip, Tetrarch of Trachonitis, died, "having reigned thirty-seven years," *i.e.* in the thirty-seventh year of his reign, in the twentieth year of Tiberius Cæsar. For, adding thirty-six complete years to the Spring of 750, we have 786, in the Spring of which, therefore, Philip's thirty-seventh year would begin; and in August of that same year 786, the twentieth year of Tiberius began.

In order to arrive at an approximate date for THE NATIVITY, we have now to consider the events recorded in the Gospels as happening between that event and the death of King Herod. These are: (1) The forty days of purification appointed by the law of Moses (Lev. xii. 1–4; Luke ii. 22). (2) The presentation in the Temple. (3) The visit of the Magi to Bethlehem. (4) The flight into Egypt and sojourn there until Herod's death (Matt. ii.). We cannot with any shade of probability suppose that the visit of Mary and Joseph to Jerusalem, publicly to present the infant Jesus in the Temple, and to offer the appointed sacrifices, took place after the visit of the Magi and their inquiry concerning the new-born King had alarmed King Herod, and "all Jerusalem with him." Therefore, even if the Wise Men from the East arrived immediately after the presentation in the Temple, JESUS was at least six weeks old when the star which they had seen in their own country shone over His birthplace. King Herod had not yet left Jerusalem, nor was he yet so prostrate with disease as to render the hypocrisy of his professed purpose, to "come and worship Him also," transparently obvious. We can, therefore, scarcely allow less than four or five weeks at the very least between the visit of the Magi and Herod's death. This, as we have seen, must have happened on or about April 1. Adding together these two periods of six weeks and four or five weeks, and deducting them from April 1, we are thrown back to the first half of January, as the latest possible date of our Saviour's birth. And it may very easily have been a week or two earlier. The festival of CHRISTMAS, therefore, although it has no historical authority,—for early Christian writers speak of the exact date of the Nativity as unknown, and Chrysostom (in A.D. 386) speaks of December 25 as a newly-instituted festival,— yet corresponds generally with the season to which the most careful calculation compels us to assign our Saviour's birth. No proof can be adduced that December 25 is the actual day. But it is no impossible date, and at all events can scarcely be far from the true anniversary.

No light is shed on the date of the Nativity by the ingenious conjecture, started by the astronomer Kepler, that the star seen by the Magi was a rare and splendid conjunction of the planets Jupiter and Saturn. St. Matthew says, that the star "went before them, till it came and stood over where the young Child was." As they were then journeying due south, this description manifestly cannot apply to any fixed star or planet, whose apparent motion in the sky would be from east to west, and which would appear as far off when the pilgrims reached Bethlehem as when they left Jerusalem. It can apply only to a meteor or luminous body moving comparatively near the earth.

A calculation has been made by Greswell, Wieseler, and others, which has a bearing on the relative ages of our Lord and of John the Baptist. The twenty-four courses into which the Jewish priesthood was divided officiated in turn for a week each. Jewish tradition states that at the destruction of the Temple (August 5, A.D. 70) the course of Joiarib had just entered office. Reckoning back from this date, it is found that the course of Abia, to which the father of John the Baptist belonged (Luke i. 5–23), was in office in the year B.C. 6 from October 3 to October 9, that is, from the twenty-first to the twenty-seventh of Tisri (*Ordo Sæcl.* p. 35; Wieseler, p. 123). Thus it was on "the last day, that great day of the feast," that the course of Abia entered office; and it may have been on that day that Zacharias' vision occurred. On October 10 Zacharias returned home. Consequently, the "sixth month" spoken of by St. Luke (i. 26) may mean the sixth month of the civil year (Adar) which ended in B.C. 5 on March 10; five calendar (Roman) months (twenty-two weeks) from the vision of Zacharias and his return home. If, in ver. 36, months of four weeks are meant, "the sixth month" would begin February 28 (counting from October 10); so that these two interpretations of the phrase practically coincide. If, following a well-known reckoning, we take "the full time" spoken of in ver. 57 to mean thirty-nine or forty weeks, or about nine calendar months, we get the first week in July for the birth of John. And if our Saviour was born about six months after His destined forerunner, mid-winter, by this independent line of reckoning, is again indicated as the date of the Nativity.

It is necessary to refer to some objections which may be advanced against the views we have arrived at, which if not satisfactorily met might seem seriously to detract from their trustworthiness. Let us, however, lay it down, here as always, as a primary maxim, that difficulties, even though our ignorance may conceal from us their true solution, cannot countervail positive evidence as to facts, if such evidence be in itself clear and conclusive. The argument from difficulties, which is one of the most favourite weapons of destructive criticism, is one of the most illusory and dangerous methods of reasoning; both because there is scarcely any conclusion as to historical fact against which a skilful and learned reasoner cannot raise formidable objections, and because ignorance can never be a basis of knowledge.

The objections in question refer (1) to the fact of the *census* recorded by St. Luke; (2) and (3) to the supposed difficulty of assigning mid-winter as the season of the Nativity.

(1) St. Luke states that, "there went out a decree from Cæsar Augustus, that all the world should be taxed,"—or, rather, should be registered or enrolled. By "the world," is meant that part of the world which acknowledged the sway of Augustus—the Empire. (Comp. Dan. iv. 1.) It is objected, 1st. That we have no account in ancient historians of any such *census orbis*, or imperial registration, under Augustus. 2dly. That an enrolment of persons and property did indeed take place under the government of Cyrenius —that is to say, P. Sulpicius Quirinus—which led to the revolt referred to by St. Luke in Acts v. 37; but this was ten years after the death of Herod, on occasion of the deposition of Archelaus (Josephus, *Ant.* xviii. 1).

It has been attempted to meet the first difficulty by understanding the word translated "the world" (Greek "oikoumenè "—"inhabited ") to refer only to the land of Palestine. Dr. Lardner (*Works*, vol. i. pp. 252-272) defends this view with great learning (including in his argument also Acts xi. 28; Matt. xxiv. 14); but, though upheld by some other weighty authorities, it is generally allowed to be untenable. The evidence, notwithstanding Lardner's strictures, is very considerable, that a census of the Roman empire did actually take place about A.U.C. 750. And it is little less than absurd to suppose that a careful historian like St. Luke would make a statement of this sort without being perfectly certain of its correctness.[1]

As regards the second objection, St. Luke's words are capable of being rendered, "this enrolment took place before Cyrenius was Governor;" but the more natural is, "This enrolment was the first" (or, this was the first enrolment), "Cyrenius being Governor;" thus distinguishing this from the later "taxing" mentioned in Acts v. 37. A German scholar, Augustus Zumpt, with immense pains and sagacity, has collected reasons for believing that Quirinus was, in fact, Governor of Syria *twice*—his *second* term of office being that referred to by Josephus, but the *first* having commenced in the latter part of B.C. 4. The difficulty is not, indeed, thus wholly removed, for it is not till after the death of Herod the Great that he is supposed to have taken the government; but it is an obvious and probable supposition that the census, begun during Herod's reign, was completed, and the official returns made, under Quirinus. St. Luke's accuracy is thus amply vindicated. Wieseler (writing before the publication of Zumpt's investigations, combines two explanations of St. Luke's words, which he translates: "This registration was the first [that was made] before Cyrenius was Governor of Syria." (See his learned and full criticism, *Eng. Trans.*, pp. 97–105; with the translator's note on the results of Zumpt's inquiries, pp. 129–135.) Dean Merivale (*History of the Romans*, vol. iv. p. 457) concludes that "the enumeration, begun or appointed under Varus, and before the death of Herod, was completed after that event by Quirinus."

[1] The proofs may be found in Greswell's *Dissertations* and Browne's *Ordo Sæclorum*, but are stated, I think, most fully and clearly in Wieseler's *Chronological Synopsis*, pp. 66–86. Wieseler likewise deals very acutely and satisfactorily with the objections drawn from the silence of Josephus, and from the statement that Joseph and Mary had to go to Bethlehem to be enrolled (pp. 86–95).

The manner in which minute and laborious inquiry thus confirms the historical trustworthiness of the Gospels, and even turns difficulties into evidence, is the best answer to the theory, supported by reckless and sweeping statements, that the four Gospels were comparatively late compositions, compiled out of fragmentary traditions towards the close of the second century. Had such been their character, they would infallibly have abounded with blunders, which it would have been a hopeless task to explain away.

(2) An objection has been raised against the view that our Saviour's birth took place in mid-winter, on the ground that the depth of winter would have been so unsuitable a season for this public registration, on account of the difficulty of journeying (comp. Matt. xxiv. 20), that it is very improbable that the Nativity can have taken place at that season. A similar objection would tell with far greater force against assigning our Lord's birth (with Mr. Greswell) to the Passover. A public registration would have been impracticable when people were travelling in myriads to Jerusalem. But at mid-winter, people would be in their homes; and though some, like Joseph and Mary, would have to travel far to their ancestral cities, the majority we may suppose would be registered in the district in which they dwelt. Moreover, neither Augustus nor Herod was likely to bestow much consideration on private convenience.

(3) It is objected, again, that shepherds could not have been "abiding in the field, keeping watch over their flocks by night," at mid-winter. It was the custom, Jewish books tell us, to drive the flocks up to the hill pastures in March, and down again in November. If, therefore, St. Luke described the shepherds and their flocks as out on those upland pastures, it would be evident that the season could not be winter. But he does not. He says, "There were shepherds in the same neighbourhood, lodging·

in the field" (passing the night out of doors), "and watching the watches of the night over their flock." The fold would need to be guarded against thieves and wolves as much in winter as in summer, if not more. Jacob (Gen. xxxi. 40) complains of his sufferings from frost as well as heat. This difficulty, therefore (which, I confess, formerly seemed to me very serious), vanishes on close scrutiny.

The view to which Dr. Geikie (vol. i. p. 150) seems half inclined, that the eclipse mentioned by Josephus may have been one which happened January 10, B.C. 1 (A.U.C. 753), is in flat contradiction to the express statement of Josephus as to the length of Herod's reign, which is the starting-point of our calculations; and Dr. Geikie, in imagining that Joseph and Mary may have lived nearly three years in Egypt, seems for the moment to have forgotten that the only reason for supposing them to have gone to Egypt in B.C. 4 is the fact of Herod's death in that year.

Two eclipses of the moon, visible in Judæa, are recorded by astronomers to have occurred in B.C. 1. But the date of Herod's death (and thus of the Nativity) depends not on the eclipse, but on the length of his reign, as carefully given by Josephus from a double date: thirty-four years from A.U.C. 717; thirty-seven years from A.U.C. 714. The eclipse merely affects the question, *where* to place Herod's death between 1 Nisan B.C. 4, and 1 Nisan B.C. 3.

It is needless to refer here to writers who have assigned much earlier dates for the birth of Christ, because from Matt. ii. 16, understanding *"from two years old and under"* to mean, according to Jewish usage, those who had entered the second year, it could not, at the utmost, have been more than a year before the visit of the Magi. Nor would an earlier date harmonize with the account of the birth and ministry of John the Baptist, or with the statement concerning our Lord's age in Luke iii. 23.

SECTION II.

THE FULNESS OF TIME.

THE true use of chronology is to *synchronize* events, and thus to throw light on their mutual bearings, so that we may be able not only to frame a comprehensive picture of the world at any given epoch, but to view its great lines of history as parts of one divinely-ordered whole—a complicated web in which every thread is employed in weaving that supreme design which we daily trace, but which God's eye alone takes in. St. Paul tells us, that, "when the fulness of the time was come, God sent forth His Son, made of a woman, made under the law" (Gal. iv. 4). When the angels announced His birth to the shepherds of Bethlehem, and sang that first Christmas song of " Glory to God in the highest, and on earth peace, goodwill toward men," a thousand years had rolled by since the building of Solomon's Temple, and more than five hundred since the second Temple was raised under Zerubbabel the Prince, Joshua the high-priest, and Haggai and Zechariah the prophets, by the Jews who had returned from their captivity in Babylon and in Assyria in obedience to the proclamation of the great conqueror Cyrus. During those five centuries three mighty revolutions had run their course, each having an important part in preparing the world for the coming of the Saviour.

First, the rise and victorious progress of the Roman Republic, and its conversion (within the memory of that generation) into an Empire, whose dominions embraced Europe within the Danube and the Rhine, Asia west of the Euphrates, Egypt, and the northern coast of Africa.

Secondly, the rise, glory, and decline of Greek philosophy, art, and literature.

THE FULNESS OF TIME. 23

Thirdly, the rise and transient splendour of Alexander's empire, built on the ruins of Greek liberty, with the formation out of its fragments of the powerful kingdoms of Syria and Egypt, of whose greatness the two great chief cities of the world after Rome — Alexandria and Antioch — were the most splendid and lasting monuments.

The Roman Empire supplied the outward conditions necessary for the rapid spread of the religion and kingdom of Christ among the nations: notably these three—Peace, Roads, and Government. War would have rendered impossible the free and frequent passage from land to land even of single missionaries of the Cross, like Paul; still more, of the scattered multitude of willing labourers who "went everywhere preaching the word." Along the great military roads which connected Rome with every corner of the empire, as well as in the merchant ships which carried on their peaceful commerce along all the shores of the Great Sea, these messengers of the kingdom of peace safely journeyed. In that age nothing could have maintained this wide-spread tranquillity, but the irresistible hand of a central despotism.

> "No war, or battle's sound
> Was heard the world around:
> The idle spear and shield were high up hung;
> The hookèd chariot stood
> Unstained with hostile blood;
> The trumpet spake not to the armèd throng;
> And kings sat still with awful eye,
> As if they surely knew their Sovran Lord was by."

Before a generation had passed, the Imperial Government was to enter upon the task of suppressing the new religion, to which end, during three centuries, its power was exerted to the uttermost. But, "in the beginning of the Gospel," we see Roman law extending its shield over the Christians, and St. Paul's

Roman citizenship saving him alike from the scourge of the soldiers of Lysias, and from the daggers of Jewish assassins. The wide, yet compact, empire of Rome embraced, we may say, the central life of mankind, with whatever of knowledge and civilization Christianity could best employ in entering upon the work of evangelizing the world. In the distant East, among the vast populations of India and China, Buddhism, founded about the time of the Babylonian captivity, was already five centuries old; elaborate systems of philosophy could boast of great antiquity; and the sacred books of the Brahmins and of the Parsees preserved relics of the primæval religion. But all this was aloof from the main stream of human life and progress, and destined no more to influence its course than, twelve centuries later, the wide conquests and splendid empire of the great Tartar monarchs. On the other hand, behind the Rhine and the Danube, in the wide wildernesses of Germany and Scandinavia, God was keeping in store the reserve force of humanity, in the Teutonic and Scandinavian nations, whose rugged freedom defied the power and was a stranger to the corruption of Rome, and was destined (five hundred years later) to pour fresh lifeblood into decaying Christendom, and to take the lead in spreading the kingdom of Christ amongst mankind.

The Jewish nation practically fell under the power of the Romans sixty years before the birth of our Lord, in consequence of their miserable civil wars. Pompey, being appealed to, entered Jerusalem, stormed the Temple, and profaned the Holy of Holies. Judæa was formally reduced to a Roman province ten years after the death of Herod the Great, on the deposition of his son Archelaus. To the Romans also, forty years after the Crucifixion, and again seventy years later (A.D. 70 and 140), God committed the tremendous task of accomplishing the judgments denounced by our Saviour against those who "knew not the day of their visitation."

To the philosophy and culture of Greece it had been given during those five preparatory centuries to carry human genius, intellect, and art to a transcendent pitch, never excelled. Those keen and subtle thinkers, who founded or moulded the various schools of Greek philosophy, anticipated in a remarkable degree the speculations of modern anti-Christian thinkers; and while they showed that "the world by wisdom knew not God," they also proved by their failure the impossibility of solving, apart from the knowledge of God, the deepest and most urgent problems of human nature. In these and in other ways, Greek culture was helping to prepare the way for the Gospel; but most of all by developing that rich, flexible, accurate, and noble language, in which (shorn, in the lapse of time, of much of its refinement and decoration, but not of its force, clearness, or majesty) the New Testament Scriptures were to become the most precious and imperishable heirloom of mankind. Meanwhile religion and morals were everywhere decaying. The devout though ignorant faith which had once lain like a preserving salt at the core of ancient paganism, was perishing under the double influence of sceptical philosophy and social luxury and corruption. Atheism was boldly professed, and, though the temples of the gods were never more splendid, the belief in their existence was dying out.

Alexander the Great said to himself, that his work was "to sow Greece over Asia;" and though his conquests and life were cut short while his vast schemes were but in the bud, and his empire was speedily broken up, yet the Greek language, learning, and civilization were so widely spread as to form a marvellous preparation for the preaching of a universal religion. To the patronage of the Greek kings of Egypt the Jews were indebted for the Greek translation of the Old Testament Scriptures, known as the Septuagint or Version of the Seventy. Alexandria, the first city in the world after Rome, became no less busy a centre of learning, philosophy, and intellectual life than of commercial activity, and was destined to exert a most powerful influence on the progress of Christian thought and belief. The influence of the Greek kingdom of Syria upon the Jewish people, on the other hand, is chiefly memorable for the intolerable oppression and insult inflicted upon them by Antiochus Epiphanes, whose attempt to substitute paganism for the worship of Jehovah roused that splendid outburst of religious patriotism, under the heroic Maccabees, which restored the national worship and for a season re-established national liberty and independence.

At the time of our Saviour's birth, the just and devout Israelites, such as were "Israelites indeed," were waiting for "the consolation of Israel," and "looked for redemption." Heathen historians bear witness to the fact, that the expectation of a universal monarch, who should spring from Judæa, prevailed throughout the East. But the prospect, as far as the Jewish nation was concerned, was dark in the extreme. The disastrous feuds of the later Maccabean chiefs had issued in placing an Edomite on David's throne, and riveting the Roman yoke on the neck of Israel. From the one sin which had proved the most fatal temptation to their forefathers, the Jews of our Saviour's day were indeed free—idolatry. It is not wonderful that the cruelties and outrages of Antiochus, and the profanation and spoliation of the Temple by Pompey and Crassus, had raised the zeal against heathenism to a fever-heat of fierce fanaticism. The disdain of other nations they repaid with still haughtier contempt. They clung with intense fervour to the hope of the coming Messiah. But, untaught by those glorious prophecies of the Old Testament which told how all nations were to become His inheritance and blessed in Him, they looked for a warlike conqueror, who should trample underfoot the Romans and all their other enemies, raise the throne of David and Solomon to far more than its ancient splendour, and enable all true Israelites to revel in worldly wealth and carnal luxury. Meantime neither the religious nor the moral character of the nation furnished any warrant for this conceit of their superiority to the heathen around and amongst them. The vivid pictures supplied by the Gospels, of the ostentatious formalism, unmeasured pride, and fierce bigotry of the Pharisees, with too many of whom devotion was but a cloak for covetousness and vice, and of the scepticism of the Sadducees, whose religion was a cold morality, are abundantly confirmed by the Talmud. The law of God, as interpreted by the Rabbins, had been overlaid with endless comments, refinements, and inferences, which converted it into that heaviest of burdens—a mountain of trifles. The natural result, with the mass of the people, who could make no pretension to Pharisaic sanctity, must have been to relax the obligation of all law. They were regarded by their spiritual teachers with insolent and heartless disdain, and wandered as sheep without a shepherd. (Comp. John vii. 49; Matt. ix. 36.) The violence with which the land was filled must have had a frightfully hardening influence on men's minds. In the terrible language of Hosea (iv. 2), "blood touched blood." Idolatry excepted, the darkest pictures painted by the Old Testament prophets of ancient Israel were realized. The practice of polygamy and of easy and frequent divorce poisoned the fountain-head of family and social life. Herod the Great, who waded through a river of blood to the throne, and spared neither wife nor son, if he fancied their murder would contribute to his safety, wrote his own epitaph, when, a few days before his death, having got together the leading men out of every village in Judæa, he imprisoned them in the circus at Jericho, and gave secret orders that they should be massacred immediately on his death; thus providing (as he imagined) that the nation, instead of rejoicing at being quit of their tyrant, should be plunged into universal mourning (Jos. *Ant.* xvii. 6: 5; *Wars*, i. 33: 8). This monstrous order was not, indeed, carried out, but Herod's crime is not thereby lessened, and the very conception of such a purpose seems fiendish. In the fearful words of Josephus (who was not lacking in either national or priestly pride), "that time was fruitful among the Jews of every kind of wickedness, leaving undone no deed of baseness; nor, if any one wished to imagine some new crime, was room left to invent it. Thus, in private and in public, all were corrupt, and they made it their ambition to outdo one another alike in impiety towards God, and in injustice towards their neighbour. The rich and the great evil-treated the multitude, and the multitude eagerly strove to destroy the rich and great: the former thirsting for power, the latter for blood and rapine." Of those who perished in the siege of Jerusalem, he says, that if the Romans had not destroyed those wretches, the city would either have been swallowed by an earthquake, or overwhelmed by a deluge, or overthrown, like Sodom, by fire from heaven; "for it bore a generation far more godless than those who so perished" (*Wars*, vii. 8: 1; v. 13: 6).

Thus the world waited for its Lord and Deliverer, but knew not for what or for whom it waited, or what was the cause and what the remedy of its measureless woes. "He was in the world, and the world was made by Him, and the world knew Him not. He came unto His own, and His own received Him not. But as many as received Him, to them gave He power to become the sons of God, even to them that believe on His name."

For fuller information on the subjects treated in

THE FULNESS OF TIME.

the foregoing sections, the reader may be referred to Josephus, *Antiquities*, books xiii.–xvii.; *Wars*, books i., ii. 1–8; Dr. N. Lardner's *Works*, vol. i.; Browne's *Ordo Sæclorum;* Wieseler's *Chronological Synopsis of the Four Gospels*, translated by the Rev. E. Venables; Conybeare and Howson's *Life and Epistles of St. Paul*, chap. i.; Neander's *Church History*, Introduction; and the learned and popular works of Dr. Farrar and Dr. Geikie.

LEADING DATES.	B.C.	A.U.C.
Rome founded	753	1
Edict of Cyrus	536	218
Temple at Jerusalem finished, under Darius	516	238
Republics of Rome and Athens established	510	244
Death of Alexander the Great	323	431
Era of Seleucidæ	312	442
Revolt of Maccabees	167	587
Jerusalem taken by Pompey	63	691
Jerusalem taken by Herod	37	717
Augustus Cæsar Emperor, having been sole ruler for three years previously	27	727
Death of Herod the Great	4	750

PART II.
THE THIRTY YEARS.

SECTION I.

INFANCY.

IT was a rude welcome that our ungrateful world offered to her Divine Lord, when, "though He was rich, yet for" our "sakes He became poor." Refused lodging in the city of David, even in the inn, cradled in a manger, receiving the homage of a few simple peasants in a stable; of two aged saints in the Temple; and of a little company of wise strangers from the remote East, whose hearts God had touched, in the house over which the wondrous star halted; He who was "born King of the Jews" had to seek safety from the murderous rage of the usurper who profaned David's throne in a sudden flight across the border of the Holy Land. Egypt, as it had been of yore the foster-nurse of Israel's two greatest deliverers —Joseph and Moses—was now to have the honour of affording an asylum to that greater Deliverer, whose name was called JESUS, because "He shall save His people from their sins."

"When the fulness of the time was come," St. Paul tells us, "God sent forth His Son, made of a woman, made under the law." In obedience, therefore, to the law of Moses, the Holy Child received, on the eighth

INFANCY.   31

day from His birth, the token of God's covenant with Abraham, and the Hebrew name " JOSHUA," for which the Gospels give the Greek form " JESUS," signifying " Jehovah [is] salvation." (Matt. i. 21 ; Luke ii. 21. Compare Numb. xiii. 16 ; Acts vii. 45.) In obedience, likewise, to the Divine law, Mary observed the prescribed forty days of seclusion ; and then, accompanied by her husband, went up to Jerusalem, for the twofold purpose of offering, on her own behalf, the appointed sacrifices, and of presenting her first-born Son before the Lord. (Lev. xii.; Ex. xiii. 2, 13, 15; xxxiv. 20; Numb. xviii. 16 ; Luke ii. 22–24.) The redemption money required by the law, due when the child was thirty days old, had probably been set aside, and was now brought by Joseph and paid into the Temple treasury. The full sacrifice ordained by the law was "a lamb of the first year for a burnt-offering "—the symbol of entire consecration—" and a young pigeon or a turtle dove for a sin-offering ; " but if the worshipper were too poor to afford a lamb, a dove or pigeon might be substituted as a burnt-offering; and with this humbler gift Mary had to content herself. These sacrifices were for the mother, not for the Child, who was Himself presented, as " a living sacrifice, holy, acceptable to God " (Rom. xii. 1). The presentation took place only in the case of a first-born son; and the Rabbins held that it must be omitted if the child had any bodily deformity or blemish, such as would unfit him, if he were a Levite, for the Temple service. We thus learn, incidentally, that the Holy Child was in body, as well as spirit, " without blemish and without spot."

Mary, with her Child and her husband, would probably reach the Temple soon after sunrise. They would enter the great Court of the Gentiles, either from the valley of Kedron, by the " Gate Shushan ; " or through one of the " Huldah gates " (*i.e.* "*weasel gates*"), in the great South Wall, which led up by subterranean steps into the Court; or by one of the western gates (Jos., *Ant.* xv. 11: 5). From the outer court they would enter the Temple properly so called through the lofty and magnificent gate called "Beautiful" (Acts iii. 2); and crossing the Court of the Women, would ascend the fifteen steps leading to "Nicanor's Gate;" passing through which, they stood in silent worship within the Altar-Court (Court of Israel, and of the Priests). In front of them was the great Altar of Sacrifice; and towering behind that, the Porch of the Sanctuary, one hundred cubits from side to side, and one hundred and twenty cubits high, built of white marble, gorgeous with golden decoration. Here stood the mothers who had come to offer sacrifice, until the priest came and sprinkled them with the atoning blood. Then the service was ended, and they must depart by another gate than that by which they entered.

Many other mothers were probably there that spring morning; but it might easily happen that Mary was the only one who had a first-born son to present before the Lord. As she was reverently bearing her precious charge, accompanied by Joseph, towards the ascent to the Altar-Court, they were met (in the Court of the Women) by two venerable personages, the saintly Simeon and the prophetess Anna, divinely commissioned to bear witness that the CHILD now to be presented before God was none other than the promised MESSIAH, the Anointed King and Deliverer of Israel. Anna (or Hannah), being of the tribe of Asher, was a representative of the ten tribes, and no doubt a Galilæan. It has been conjectured that Simeon (or Simon) was no other than the son of the great Hillel, and father of the famous Gamaliel. But the dates do not tally. For Simon ben Hillel lived for more than thirty years after this, succeeding his father as Nasi or President of the Sanhedrin in A.D. 10, and being succeeded by Gamaliel in A.D. 30.

Thus the voice of inspired prophecy, silent for ages, awoke again in Israel at the advent of Him to whom all the prophets bare witness. The infant son of Zacharias and Elisabeth, by whose lips, thirty years later, it was to utter a testimony and a warning that would make the ears of the whole nation tingle, had doubtless been presented in the Temple in like manner some six months earlier.

If, as we have seen reason to conclude, the birth of Jesus took place within a few days, earlier or later, of New Year's Day, B.C. 4, the presentation in the Temple must have been about the middle of February. The visit of the Magi, we may suppose (though for this we have no distinct note of time) to have occurred not long—perhaps immediately—after. The flight into Egypt would thus be about the end of February. Before the tyrant was aware that the Magi had disobeyed his command, Joseph, warned of God, had fled across the frontier, to seek a safe retreat amongst his fellow-countrymen in Egypt, where the Jewish settlers were numerous and wealthy. Possibly, some vague reports of the prophecies uttered by Simeon and Anna, or of words privately spoken by them to "all them that looked for redemption in Jerusalem" (Luke ii. 38), as well as the startling question of the Magi, may have contributed to the excitement which led to that rash attack on the golden eagle in the Temple, for which the Rabbins and their adherents paid so dearly. The cruel execution of the Rabbins, it will be remembered, took place on March 13.

The stay of the Holy Family in Egypt was probably brief. Joseph, we may be sure, would lose no time in obeying the Divine command: "Arise, and take the young Child and His mother, and go into the land of Israel: for they are dead which sought the young Child's life" (Matt. ii. 20). Therefore, since Herod's death took place shortly before the

Passover, it was probably at the very season at which the children of Israel went forth from Egypt, that the ancient prophetic word received a new accomplishment: "Out of Egypt have I called My Son." As the travellers reached the frontier, they were met by tidings "that Archelaus did reign in Judæa in the room of his father Herod,"—accompanied, probably, with an account of the terrible massacre, by which he had given a proof that he inherited his father's bloodthirsty spirit, and an earnest of the kind of ruler he would prove. If, as seems not improbable, Joseph and Mary had entertained the notion that it would be their duty to bring up the Child around whose birth such marvels and such predictions had clustered, either in Jerusalem or at Bethlehem, any such purpose was at once dispelled. Avoiding Judæa, they hastened to seek safety under the milder rule of Herod Antipas, Tetrarch of Galilee, and returned to their old home, Nazareth. There, unlike his illustrious kinsman and forerunner, John the son of Zacharias, whose lonely childhood in the home of his aged parents, and doubtless early orphanage, prepared him for a solitary and severe life, and who "was in the deserts till the day of his showing unto Israel;" the Child Jesus was to grow up to manhood in the midst of home affection and family duties, with the faces and voices of brothers and sisters around Him; no stranger to the privations and trials of lowly life, nor yet unacquainted with the pure joys of childhood. Among the flowery hills of Nazareth, far from the splendour of courts, the tumult and corruption of great cities, and the gorgeous rites of the Temple worship, amid the simple surroundings of an artisan's home, "the Child grew, and waxed strong in spirit, filled" (or "becoming full"—increasingly filled) "with wisdom: and the grace of God was upon Him" (Luke ii. 40).

Great stress has been laid by critics on the difference between Luke's narrative and Matthew's regarding the infancy of our Lord. Even the devout and scholarly Alford writes quite wildly in his note on Luke ii. 39. But silence is not contradiction. One of the most remarkable features of Scripture history (alike O. T. and N. T.), is the absolute silence in which matters are passed over which are not essential to the writer's purpose. If St. Luke had seen (as I believe he must have seen) St. Matthew's account, that was all the more reason for his confining his own narrative to what had been expressly communicated to him,—no doubt on the authority of our Lord's mother, and probably by St. John, with whom she resided. These two chapters (excepting vers. 1–4 of ch. i.) have every appearance of having been first composed in Hebrew. The conjecture that they were originally from the pen of the Beloved Apostle, suggests an interesting comment on St. Luke's statement (i. 2) concerning "eye-witnesses, and ministers of the word;" as well as on the omission in the opening of St. John's Gospel of all reference to our Lord's earthly parentage, birthplace, or early life, coupled with the indications (ch. i. 43; ii. 1, 12; iii. 43–5) that these matters were familiar to his readers.

SECTION II.

LIFE AT NAZARETH.

NAZARETH, often incorrectly described as a "village," but in the Gospels always spoken of as a "city"—that is, a walled town, was wonderfully chosen as the retreat, obscure though not lonely, in which the Son of God was to learn and practise that part of His human experience which lay in private duty and patient waiting until His "hour" came (John ii. 4). Had the Evangelists been inventing

NAZARETH.

or embellishing a legend, in place of relating with scrupulous fidelity the plain facts, they would certainly not have represented the Messiah as spending His whole life except the last three years in a town so utterly unknown to fame that it is not once named in the Old Testament, and of such evil repute that it seemed incredible that "any good thing" could come out of Nazareth. Approached from the south by a single road through a steep gorge, the mountain valley on the sunny side of which the town is built is completely encircled by hills, shutting it in from the rest of the world; but from whose tops the eye sweeps a wide and glorious panorama; to the W., Carmel and the Great Sea; to the S., the great Plain of Esdraelon and Mount Gilboa; to the S.E., Mount Tabor; to the N.E. and N., the hills of Upper Galilee (among which the lake lies hidden); and in the far distance "the snowy dome of Hermon." The air of this lofty region is pure and healthful. The neighbourhood is noted for the abundance and beauty of wild flowers. Without accepting the astonishing statement of Josephus that the smallest village of Galilee had not fewer than fifteen thousand inhabitants, we may suppose Nazareth in the time of our Lord to have had a considerable population. But its inhabitants probably were but little affected by the stream of commerce and military movement which flowed at no great distance to the west along the Roman road from Sepphoris and the coast to Jerusalem and the south. With few ideas beyond the circle of their own hills, they were narrow-minded, bigoted, rude, and turbulent, and, as such people are, easily offended. Perhaps, on the other hand, they may have been free from some of the corrupting influences which haunt wealthy cities and the courts of princes.

Ten years had passed since the Holy Family took up their abode at Nazareth,—years, we may believe, of peaceful home happiness, where religion hallowed duty, and duty strengthened love—when tidings reached the mountain valley of a great political revolution; not, indeed, affecting Galilee, yet in which every Israelite must have taken a profound interest. Archelaus, accused to Augustus by the leading men of Judæa and Samaria of intolerable misgovernment and tyranny, was deposed and banished, and his dominions annexed to the Roman province of Syria. A Roman governor, styled "Procurator," was placed over Judæa and Samaria, with Cæsarea as the seat of government. Thus "the sceptre" visibly "departed from Judah." Herod's rule had in a sense represented the national dominion of the Maccabees. He was "King of the Jews;" and although the throne of David was never restored after the Captivity, yet the pre-eminence of the royal tribe was recognized in the fact that the whole nation of Israel accepted the name of "Jews," or "Judahites." But now supreme political power finally passed out of Jewish hands; a heathen Roman was supreme magistrate in Jerusalem itself, and the Sanhedrin had to confess that they had lost the power of capital punishment, and had "no king but Cæsar" (John xviii. 31; xix. 12, 15). A new token was thus given that the time of Messiah had arrived.

This great revolution might at first appear to be easily as well as quickly accomplished. But it planted germs of deep and wide-spread resentment, and sowed the seed of troubles which largely contributed to the final ruin of the nation. The nation, however politically divided, was religiously one; and Jerusalem and the Temple were the centre of that unity. Although Galilee was not politically affected by the change, all pious and patriotic Galilæans would feel as bitterly as the inhabitants of Jerusalem the humiliation of having the Temple and the Holy City placed under the control of a heathen foreigner, the agent of Roman despotism. The test question propounded to Jesus twenty years later,—"Is it lawful to give tribute to Cæsar or no?"—was one which He must often have heard debated by excited groups of Galilæans at Nazareth. Coponius, the newly appointed Procurator, was accompanied into Judæa by Cyrenius (or Quirinus), Governor of Syria, who came to take possession of the effects of Archelaus, and to arrange for the collection of taxes, which were thenceforth to be paid into the Roman exchequer. The leading Jews were inclined peaceably to submit. But Judas the Galilæan (or Gaulonite) denounced the impost as an intolerable badge of servitude, boldly maintained that God's chosen people could acknowledge no sovereign but God, and roused a fierce spirit of revolt against the yoke of Rome. It was to this movement that Gamaliel referred, in the speech recorded by St. Luke (Acts v. 37). Josephus reckons the followers of Judas as a fourth Jewish sect,—the other three being the Pharisees, Sadducees, and Essenes (*Ant.* xviii. 1; xx. 5: 2; *Wars*, ii. 8).

The veil of reverent silence drawn by the Evangelists over the childhood, youth, and early manhood of our Saviour is lifted but once, to relate His visit, when twelve years of age, with His parents, to the Holy City, to keep the Passover (Luke ii. 41–52). The incident sheds a beautiful gleam of light on the punctual observance, in the home of Jesus, of the Divine law: "His parents went to Jerusalem every year at the feast of the Passover."

We are not expressly told that this was the first visit Jesus paid to the City and Temple; but that is the impression conveyed by the narrative. At twelve years old a Jewish boy began to take his place as an Israelite, and learn (by degrees) to fast; and to apply himself to some trade or calling (*Lightfoot*). At this time two years had elapsed since Judæa lost its nationality, and was placed under heathen rulers.

The Evangelist briefly tells us that Jesus returned

with Joseph and Mary to Nazareth, "and was subject unto them;" adding that He "increased in wisdom and stature, and in favour with God and man" (Luke ii. 51, 52). Without giving the rein to an over-bold curiosity, there are some points regarding this period of our Lord's history of which we may feel certain. Nazareth must have possessed a spacious synagogue, and a good public school. Josephus assures us, that the one thing on which the Jews bestowed the most anxious care, was the education of their children (*Against Ap.* i. 12).

According to the Rabbins, a boy was to be sent to school at six years of age; but at five his father was to begin instructing him in the Scriptures,—teaching him, that is, not to read, but to recite passages by rote. At ten, he must begin to learn the oral law, and at fifteen the rabbinical interpretations and inferences. This we must understand to be the rabbinical ideal of a complete education, rather than a description of the actual training of the bulk of Jewish boys. But we may at all events be assured that "from a child" our Saviour learned and knew those "Holy Writings," which He was afterwards to quote and expound as no other teacher could. Regular attendance at the Synagogue services on the Sabbath was a matter of course, probably also at the briefer services on Mondays and Thursdays. When He had reached manhood, it was "His custom" (as we learn from Luke iv. 16) to take His turn among the public readers of the appointed lessons in the Synagogue service; possibly also in leading the prayers of the congregation. We may infer, however, from the amazement which His address in the Synagogue at Nazareth excited, on the occasion described by St. Luke (iv. 16, ff.), that He refrained from public teaching and exhortation until the time arrived for Him to teach "with authority, and not as the Scribes."[1]

[1] The reading of the Law on the Sabbath (Acts xiii. 15, 27;

We have our Lord's own authority for interpreting the Fifth Commandment as involving the duty of a son to contribute according to his ability to the support and comfort of his parents (Matt. xv. 4–6). In this, as in all other duties, we can have no doubt that He "left us an example, that we should walk in His steps." That He wrought with His own hands at Joseph's handicraft is indicated by His being known at Nazareth not only as "the Son of the carpenter," but as "Jesus the Carpenter" (Mark vi. 3; compare Matt. xiii. 55; John vi. 42). From the absence of any mention of Joseph in the history after the time when Jesus was twelve years of age, and from the manner in which the mother and brethren of Jesus are spoken of in the Gospels, it appears probable that she was early left a widow. This accounts for the Nazarenes speaking of our Lord as *"the Son of Mary"* (Mark vi. 3). There is, however, no ground for the notion that Joseph was already an elderly man when he first brought home "his espoused wife" to Nazareth.

We cannot help wishing to know what was the exact position which Jesus occupied during those long years at Nazareth. Was it that of an only son, an eldest son, or a youngest son? The reply depends on the answer to another question,—Who were the "brethren" of our Lord, repeatedly referred to in the Gospels and in St. Paul's Epistles? This question has excited eager and learned controversy, chiefly on account of the value which in later times came to be attached to a life of perpetual maidenhood, which renders the supposition repugnant and even shocking to many minds, that our Lord's mother ever had any

xv. 21) was distributed among seven readers (provided so many duly qualified persons were present), the first of whom was to be a Priest, the second a Levite, the rest Israelites; and the last of the seven read also the lesson from the Prophets. See Dr. Ginsburg's elaborate articles, "Education," "Synagogue," and "Haphtora," in *Cycl. of Bib. Lit.*

other child than "her first-born Son" (Matt. i. 25). But for this sentiment,—wholly foreign to Jewish ideas—perhaps no one would have ever doubted that "His brethren, James, and Joses, and Simon, and Judas, and His sisters" (Matt. xiii. 55, 56; Mark vi. 3), were younger brothers and sisters of our Lord,—children of Joseph and Mary. Two methods have been invented of avoiding this conclusion. One hypothesis (maintained by Jerome), is, that these brethren and sisters were cousins of our Lord. No doubt Hebrew usage permits such a use of the terms; but the hypothesis rests on no evidence, and appears inconsistent with the manner in which these brethren and sisters are associated with our Lord's mother. (See Mark iii. 21, 31; Acts i. 14.) Any explanation which identifies any of these brethren with their namesakes among the twelve, seems refuted by the express declaration of St. John (vii. 5)—" Neither did His brethren believe in Him." The other view (expounded with exhaustive learning by Bishop Lightfoot [1]) has nothing in it violently improbable; namely, that the brothers and sisters of Jesus were children of Joseph by a former wife. The objection to this view, which will strike some minds as very grave, and others as unimportant, is, that in this case, Mary's Son must have held the place of the youngest child in a large family, and could have no pretension to represent Joseph as the heir of Joseph's line, which is the impression naturally conveyed by the genealogy in Matt. i. The question is one regarding which, in lieu of positive evidence, our view will be very much determined by personal feeling. Some will not endure to think of the Virgin Mother as ever descending—as they account it—to the cares of ordinary motherhood. Others will delight to think of "the Child Jesus," as having been for a season the only Son and sole light

[1] In a Dissertation (Diss. ii.) appended to his *Commentary on Galatians*.

and treasure of that humble home; but in later years, as the Elder Brother, shedding the light of His sinless holiness and perfect love on the first footsteps of the band of brothers and sisters who, as time went on, filled the home; the mainstay of the household under the burden of growing care, and the head of the family after Joseph's death.

During the thirty years of our Saviour's abode at Nazareth, Coponius, the first Roman Procurator of Judæa, was succeeded by M. Ambivius, Annius Rufus, Valerius Gratus, and Pontius Pilate. Gratus, during his eleven years of rule, deposed Annas, who had been made high-priest by Cyrenius, and appointed to that office (by an exercise of sheer despotism), in succession, Ishmael, Eleazar, Simon, and Joseph Caiaphas (Jos. *Ant.* xviii. 2: 2). The Emperor Augustus died, and was succeeded by Tiberius (A.D. 14). Herod the Tetrarch built a city "in the best part of Galilee, on the Lake of Gennesareth," which, in honour of the emperor, he named Tiberias. He also fortified Sepphoris, and made it his capital. Philip, Tetrarch of Iturea, rebuilt Panias, by the source of Jordan, and named it Cæsarea (called Cæsarea Philippi, to distinguish it from the more famous city on the coast, built by his father). He also raised the village of Bethsaida to the rank of a city, and named it Julias (Jos. *Ant.* xviii. 2 : 1).

Imagination may strive to draw aside the veil which inspiration has drawn over the life of our Saviour, until He "began to be about thirty years of age" (Luke iii. 23). For some minds the attempt will have a strong fascination; to others it will be repulsive and irreverent; and perhaps neither ought to judge the other. But faith and love must never lose sight of the lessons taught in the very silence of those years;—most marvellous in this, that nothing marvellous is recorded of them. Goodness was so unvarying, duty so evenly fulfilled, the lustre of holiness so mild and steady, that brothers and sisters, and rude Nazarene neighbours came to take it all as matter of course, and discerned in it nothing more than human. When at last the disguise was laid aside, and the Prophet-King of Israel, the promised Messiah, stood revealed, they could still only stupidly ask—"Is not this Jesus the Carpenter?"

Before our Redeemer entered on that path which was for Him alone, He hallowed the common path, and took into His heart the experience of common life. Ten times as much of life as He occupied in His public ministry, He spent in private life; working no miracle, preaching no sermon, initiating no public movement. The Divine ideal of perfect holiness, in childhood, youth, and manhood, was realized during thirty years in a life of obscure privacy, mechanical toil, and home affection and duty.

SECTION III.

THE EVE OF THE MINISTRY.

NOT with public acclaim and royal pomp, nor yet with any dazzling outburst of miraculous power, did the long-promised Son of David, who was to "save His people from their sins," emerge from the deep obscurity of His life at Nazareth, to assume His destined place and work before the eyes and in the hearts of men; yet not without due and solemn announcement. The voice of Prophecy, silent during four centuries, awoke at His approach. The Evangelist Mark (in perfect accord with the other three Gospels) thus records "the beginning of the Gospel of Jesus Christ, the Son of God; as it is written in the Prophets, Behold I send My Messenger before Thy face, which shall prepare Thy way before Thee.

The voice of one crying in the wilderness, Prepare ye the way of the Lord, make His paths straight. John did baptize in the wilderness, and preach the baptism of repentance for the remission of sins" (Mark i. 1–4). The Evangelist Luke states with unusual fulness the date of this preparatory ministry: "In the fifteenth year of the reign of Tiberius Cæsar, ... the word of God came unto John the son of Zacharias in the wilderness" (Luke iii. 1, 2). Singularly enough, this very exactness is a source of difficulty. Augustus Cæsar died, and was succeeded by Tiberius, in August A.D. 14. Reckoning from this date, the fifteenth year of Tiberius was from August, A.D. 28, to August, A.D. 29. This would give us the spring of A.D. 29 for the Passover following our Lord's baptism, at which He cleansed the Temple; and (as will presently be shown) the early part of that year for His baptism. But this does not fit with the date which on other grounds we are led to assign to the beginning of our Lord's ministry,—viz., A.D. 27. These grounds are briefly as follows.

(1) According to Luke iii. 23, Jesus was about thirty years of age at His baptism. (There is a difficulty, concerning which scholars are not agreed, regarding the meaning of the word "*beginning,*" and the exact reading of the text; but this does not affect the general sense.) If we have been correct in fixing the Nativity about the beginning (a little before or after) of B.C. 4, then in the spring of A.D. 29 our Lord would be more than *thirty-two* years of age.

(2) At the Passover at which Jesus began His public ministry, the rebuilding of the Temple had been going on during forty-six years (John ii. 20). Now the rebuilding of the Temple was begun by Herod the Great in the eighteenth year of his reign. (See Jos., *Ant.* xv. 11 : 1.) Herod's eighteenth year was from 1st Nisan of A.U.C. 734, to the same time A.U.C. ʼ735. Therefore, adding forty-five complete

years, at the Passover (*i.e.* Nisan 15th to 21st) in A.U.C. 780 (A.D. 27), forty-six regnal years had elapsed, and the forty-seventh had just begun, from the year in which the rebuilding commenced.

(3) The date A.D. 27 harmonizes with the view strongly established on other grounds (to be hereafter set forth) that our Lord's ministry occupied three years, and that the Crucifixion took place A.D. 30.

Although it is necessary thus fully to state this difficulty, since it affects the entire scheme of Gospel chronology, the solution is simple and satisfactory. The reign of Tiberius as *sole* emperor began at the death of Augustus; but he had been *joint* emperor with Augustus—a sort of vice-emperor—for two years previously. The word used by St. Luke, translated "reign," by no means implies sole empire, but applies with perfect accuracy to this share in the government, which had special reference to the provinces. Insomuch that, had St. Luke spoken of A.D. 27 as "the *thirteenth* year of the government of Tiberius," his critics might have taxed him with ignorance of this association of Tiberius with Augustus in the imperial sovereignty. With this explanation, both the Evangelist's chronology and his phraseology are seen to be perfectly accurate. We therefore understand "the fifteenth year" of Tiberius to have begun in August A.D. 26. And we may with great probability suppose that "the word of the Lord came to John," and he began his public ministry, about the close of the summer or the beginning of autumn, shortly before the time when, at the signal of "the early rains," the ploughman and the sower go forth to their work. The ministry of John had as its

The half-year from the autumn of A.D. 26 to the spring of A.D. 27 seems an ample space of time. Nothing like John's preaching had been heard for centuries. His pungent rebukes of public and private sin, his call to immediate repentance, in view of coming judgment—"the axe at the root"—and his announcement that the kingdom of God was at hand, stirred the heart of the nation to its depth. "All men counted John, that he was a prophet indeed" (Mark xi. 32), and "mused in their hearts of John, whether he were the Christ, or not" (Luke iii. 15). The public agitation and expectation arose to their highest pitch when, in reply to a formal inquiry from the Sanhedrin whether he were the Christ, or the prophet Elijah, and, if not, what his baptism and mission meant, he replied that he was the "Voice" foretold by Isaiah (xl. 3), preparing the way of the Lord; and that the Mightier One was even already among them who would baptize with the Holy Spirit, and with the fire of Divine judgment. (Matt. iii. 1–12; Mark i. 5–8; Luke iii. 1–18; John i. 6–8, 15–28).

The "Wilderness of Judæa" (Matt. iii. 1) is the name applied by geographers to that arid and barren tract of country (about forty miles in length with an average breadth of nine) which slopes steeply towards the Dead Sea from the mountain ridge which rises in the Mount of Olives 2,665 feet, at Hebron 3,546 feet, or on the average about 3,300 feet above the sea level. The surface of the Dead Sea lies nearly 1,300 feet below that level. The steep slopes and cliffs of bare limestone are furrowed by deep, rugged chasms rather than valleys; and scarcely any tokens of life, animal or vegetable, soften the frightful desolation and utter solitude. In such a region, "without trees or grass, or stream, or fountain," it is evident that not even "locusts and wild honey" (Matt. iii. 4) could be found, nor yet water. John could not have spent in such a region the years during which he " was in the deserts till the day of his shewing unto Israel" (Luke i. 80). We must seek the scene both of his hermit life and of the opening of his public ministry either nearer the banks of Jordan, where it enters the Dead Sea, or amid the mountain glens, where shepherds wandered with their flocks (Luke xv. 4; 1 Sam. xvii. 28); and where, when the early or the latter rains "drop upon the pastures of the wilderness," "the little hills rejoice on every side." Emerging from these pastoral solitudes, the Preacher "came into all the country about Jordan, preaching the baptism of repentance for the remission of sins." In the following spring we find him at "Bethabara beyond Jordan," and at "Ænon near to Salim" (John i. 28; iii. 23). For "Bethabara" the oldest MSS., and modern editors, read "Bethania." The traditional site (the crossing-place of the children of Israel under Joshua, near Jericho) appears irreconcilable, on account of its distance from Galilee, with John ii. 1, compared with i. 29, 35, 43. But "Bethania" and "Bethabara" may both have been in use, the former as the name of the locality, the latter of the ford or ferry; and recent research has discovered a ford still called "Abârah," which is within a day's journey of Cana, and is therefore very probably the place where our Saviour was pointed out by John to his disciples, possibly also the scene of His baptism.

The time of our Lord's baptism may be approximately fixed by reckoning back from the Passover. Immediately after He was baptized (Mark i. 12) Jesus spent forty days in the desert. It seems to have been immediately after His return from the scene of the temptation that He was pointed out by John to his disciples, as narrated in John i. 29. For the events recorded in verses 35-51; chap. ii. 1-13, we must allow two or three weeks. We have thus not less than eight or nine weeks to deduct from the date of the Passover, which in A.D. 27 fell on April 9. Therefore our Lord's baptism cannot have been later, but may have been earlier than the first fortnight of February, soon after He had completed His thirtieth year.

The hour had arrived for the calm, patient, obscure life at Nazareth, so sublime in its perfect simplicity and lowliness, to end. The great crises of life often arrive silently. Noiseless, unmarked, the dial-hand reaches the hour whose stroke will echo through the world to the end of time. As Jesus stepped forth from His mother's dwelling, and took the familiar path down the pass, the snow may have been still lying on the hill-tops; but in the great plain to the south, and in the warm valley of the Jordan, the olive and other trees were already bursting into leaf, the meadows thick with flowers, and the fields green with young corn. But who that saw the Son of Mary pass on His lonely way could have guessed that the springtide of the world's regeneration was waiting on His steps? Even to His prophet-herald, John, He was personally unknown until the secret Divine premonition and the corresponding miraculous token revealed to him "the Son of God" (John i. 31-34).

Considering the meaning of John's baptism, and the public confession of sin which it required, it might have seemed superfluous, not to say inconsistent, for one "who knew no sin" to submit to it. But Jesus Himself explained the reason which made this submission wise and obligatory on Him; and, while bearing testimony to the Divine mission of His forerunner, He was thus, even as on the cross, "numbered with the transgressors."

The locality of the forty days' fast, and of the temptation, cannot be determined. The awful mountain solitudes of "the wilderness of Judah," already described, present as fitting a scene as can be imagined.

But some countenance is given to the conjecture that, like Elijah, our Saviour was Divinely led into the wilderness of Horeb, by the fact that on His return we find Him beyond Jordan (John i. 28, 29).

During those six mysterious weeks of seclusion and awful spiritual conflict, the breath and touch of spring had passed over the Holy Land. As "He that should come" emerges into human sight and converse, all nature seems to welcome Him. "The field" is "joyful, and all that is therein," and "all the trees of the wood rejoice before the Lord: for He cometh, for He cometh to judge the earth: He shall judge the world with righteousness, and the people with His truth" (Ps. xcvi. 12, 13). The beloved disciple has painted for us in unfading colours the opening scenes of our Saviour's ministry, as they lived in his own memory. (John i. 29). Jesus is walking on the eastern bank of Jordan, already swollen with the melting snows of Hermon, for barley harvest is at hand. The great preacher points out to his disciples, in that calm solitary figure, "The Lamb of God, who taketh away the sin of the world." Two of them, promptly acting on this testimony, seek at once to place themselves under the teaching of the new Prophet. One of the two was Andrew, famous only for the influence exerted by his example and testimony on his brother Simon, for whom was destined the foremost place of service and honour in the kingdom which their master John had announced as at hand. The other, not expressly named, was doubtless "the disciple whom Jesus loved," the Evangelist John; probably a near kinsman of our Lord, and one of the choicest spirits not merely of that nation or age, but of the Church of God and of the human race.[1]

---

[1] The belief that St. John was a first cousin of our Lord rests on the interpretation of John xix. 25, compared with Matt. xxvii. 56, and Mark xv. 40. It is very commonly supposed that the words "His mother's sister" refer to

With a few simple, kindly, yet heart-searching words, Jesus attracts to Himself first these three, then two more—Philip of Bethsaida, and his friend Nathanael of Cana.[1] All five were men of Galilee, and all, we may assume, disciples of John. The attraction was strong enough to induce them to accompany Jesus in recrossing Jordan into Galilee. Yet how little would they imagine that the tie thus gently, almost imperceptibly, knit was to bind them in life-long service, and in union over which death would have no power, and was the obscure germ of a movement destined to subdue and regenerate the world (John i. 35–51).

We find no indication that Jesus had any intention of returning to the home at Nazareth. On the following day we find Him at Cana, an invited guest at a wedding, where His mother seems to have taken the place of house-mistress or hostess. Possibly bridegroom or bride may have been one of the brothers or sisters of Jesus. The wedding party were probably all kinsfolk or near friends; and as Andrew and Simon were partners with Zebedee's sons (Luke v. 10),

"Mary the wife of Cleophas" ("the mother of James and Joses"); but it is far more natural to understand *four* women to be spoken of, and that the sister of our Lord's mother was Salome "the mother of Zebedee's children." It is very unlikely that Mary, the mother of Jesus, had a sister of the same name; and it quite accords with St. John's suppression of his own name that he should refer to his own mother in this manner. This view throws a beautiful light both on the special love of the Master for this one disciple, and on John xix. 26, 27.

[1] There seems no room to doubt the received opinion that Nathanael was the same with the Apostle Bartholomew, who is always named in the lists of Apostles in conjunction with Philip. "Bartholomew" is simply a surname—"son of Tholmai" (or Talmai—2 Sam. iii. 3). In John xxi. 2 we find Nathanael in company with at least four (probably six) of the twelve; and we can scarcely be wrong in inferring that this "Israelite indeed" was of their number.

Philip a fellow-townsman, and Nathanael his intimate friend, we may easily account for these also being "called to the marriage," without supposing that they were invited expressly as disciples of Jesus (John ii. 1-11).

Our Lord's FIRST MIRACLE, wrought on such an occasion, in such company, upon the request of His mother, may well be regarded as a gracious leave-taking of the old home-life—a parting gleam shed on it—attended as it was with a respectful but unmistakable intimation that parental authority over Him was now a thing of the past. Unostentatious and genial as it was, the miracle was transcendently marvellous. Jesus "manifested forth His glory, and His disciples believed on Him." This private beginning of miracles was in harmony with the private informal beginning of our Lord's ministry. But privacy—except such as He could snatch by night, under the shelter of some cliff or tree—was soon to be at an end for Him. Having gone down to Capernaum in company with His mother and His brethren, and sojourned there "not many days," Jesus, like all devout Jews who were not disabled by some weighty hindrance, went up to Jerusalem to keep the Passover (John ii. 12, 13. April 9-16, A.D. 27).

During this feast Jesus publicly assumed the character and authority of a prophet, or "teacher come from God," by denouncing, and for the time putting down the market and exchange held in the great outer court surrounding the Temple, known as "the Court of the Gentiles." St. John's Gospel not simply narrates this incident as occurring at this time, but expressly assigns the date (ii. 20). The three other Gospels narrate a similar exercise of prophetic authority and zeal for His Father's house, at the closing Passover of our Lord's ministry. Only a desire to find discrepancies will lead any one to see one here. The Jewish authorities might well feel abashed as well as enraged to find themselves charged with profaning that sanctuary, reverence for which was their chief pride. But their contempt for all other nations rendered it impossible for them to feel that a yard polluted by the presence of Gentiles could be profaned by beasts and birds destined for sacrifice, or by the exchange of sacred for heathen coin. An abuse so profitable was sure to re-establish itself; and the same reasons which made this cleansing of the sanctuary the most fitting manifestation of Christ's authority and character when He " suddenly came to His Temple," made it also most fitting that He should at the close of His ministry repeat this solemn public protest against the disobedience, formalism, and ungodliness of both rulers and people. (John ii. 13–22).

N.B.—This Part (Part II.) includes Matt. i.–iv. 11; Mark i.; Luke i.–iv. 13; John i.–ii. 22.

PART III.
THE MINISTRY.

SECTION I.

FIRST YEAR. (A.D. 27, 28 = 780, 781 A.U.C.)

THAT unprecedented and startling exercise of prophetic authority and holy zeal with which our Lord announced His entrance on His public ministry in Jerusalem—the cleansing of the Temple—suggests some questions of deep interest. Are we to explain the unresisting submission of the dealers, and the tacit acquiescence of the authorities, as produced by an exercise of miraculous power, or as the natural result of that innate authority which characterizes born leaders of men, and which we must suppose the Lord Jesus to have possessed in the highest degree? The answer probably is, that Jesus was a miraculous Person, whom it was impossible to approach without being conscious of being in the presence of One who towered above the stature of ordinary manhood; and that in regard to His actions, no sharp line between the natural and the miraculous can be drawn. When He taught, it was "as having authority, and not as the Scribes" (Matt. vii. 29). When He said, "Follow Me," men felt as though an invisible hand were irresistibly laid on them, and forsook all to obey Him.

When the enraged Nazarenes seized and dragged Him to the verge of the precipice, "He passing through the midst of them went His way." When He stepped forward to meet the armed party which came to arrest Him in Gethsemane, "they went backward, and fell to the ground" (Luke iv. 30; John xviii. 6).

No authentic description has come down to us of the personal appearance of Jesus. Isaiah's well-known prediction (liii. 2) has often been supposed to imply that it was mean and unsightly; and this repulsive notion has been justified as appropriate to our Saviour's humiliation. But the prophecy is much more reasonably interpreted as pointing to the absence of that royal pomp and worldly splendour with which Jewish fancy and expectation arrayed the Messiah,—to "His kingdom, as possessing in the eyes of men no beauty, glory, or magnificence" (*Calvin*). His stupendous public labours, and long journeys on foot, coupled with the fact that, after spending the day in toil, bodily and mental, which might well be deemed exhausting. He often found refreshment, not in sleep, but in prayer, plainly betoken a vigorous frame, proof alike against noontide heat and night dews, matured by wholesome labour and simple living in the pure hill air of Nazareth. His voice could be heard by thousands of persons in the open air, and could endure the strain of public speaking for hours together. A perfectly sinless life, unceasing communion with God, perfect mental and bodily health, and a perfect balance of all intellectual and moral faculties, ruled and inspired by love such as no other heart can have room for, must on all ordinary physiognomic principles have produced not only

"A countenance wherein did meet
Sweet records, promises as sweet,"

but a presence absolutely unique in nobleness and graciousness. When to all this we add the consideration that in Him dwelt "all the fulness of the Godhead bodily," we can scarcely err in concluding that the pre-eminent characters of His countenance were those which painters have most failed to represent, — majesty and insight: an eye that pierced men's souls, and looked into eternity; and a more than kingly aspect of authority, which made it the natural impulse of those who approached Him to fall at His feet and worship. (Matt. viii. 2; ix. 18; xiv. 33; xv. 25; Mark v. 6; John ix. 38.) Yet His presence attracted even more than it overawed. Children gathered fearlessly round Him, and ran at His call into His arms. Despised and miserable outcasts felt that He alone of all men would not spurn them or shrink from them. Publicans and sinners drew near to Him. The poor, the brokenhearted, the guilty, felt drawn by the irresistible charm of love, truth, and sympathy, when He bade them come unto Him, that they might find rest to their souls. (Mark ix. 36; Matt. xviii. 2; Luke vii. 37; xv. 1; Matt. xi. 19, 28-30.)

Unlike the ancient prophets, Jesus, from the very outset of His mission, entered into no relations with the priesthood, the Sanhedrin, or the national authorities in any form, any more than with Herod, the ruler of Galilee, or with the imperial government. In this respect the contrast, even with John the Baptist's attitude, is remarkable and instructive. John's faithful rebuke of Herod's wickedness, which in the end cost him his life, was only the sequel of many warnings and counsels addressed by him to the Tetrarch of Galilee; "for Herod feared John, knowing that he was a just man and an holy, and observed him; and when he heard him, he did many things, and heard him gladly" (Mark vi. 20). Contrast with this our Saviour's deliberate avoidance of Herod, indicated by such passages as Luke ix. 7-9; xiii. 31, 32; xxiii. 8. The ministry of Jesus was addressed to individuals ("every man," John vi. 44, 45; Mark vii. 14) and to the people—"the lost sheep of the house of Israel" (Matt. xv. 24). In the death of Christ, compared with that of His forerunner, we see this contrast reversed. The murder of John was a simple act of personal tyranny, to gratify private revenge; the death of Jesus was the public act of the Jewish authorities, to which they strove to give the colour of law and justice, as well as of public expediency (John xi. 47-50; xix. 7-12); sanctioned by the voice of the nation, as represented by the multitude assembled in Jerusalem at the Passover (Matt. xxvii. 20-25).

On His disciples Jesus enforced the duty of loyal submission to the nation rulers, as appointed to administer the Divine law (Matt. xxiii. 1-3). At the same time He unsparingly denounced the corruption and perversion (under the guise of interpretation) of the written law by the oral law, and warned His disciples that the time was at hand when they would have to choose between submission to earthly rulers, Jewish or heathen, and allegiance to Himself: or, in other words, between obedience to men and obedience to God. (See Matt. xv. 3-9, 14; xvi. 12; xxiii. 16-34; John xvi. 2; comp. Acts iv. 19; v. 29.) As they were not Rabbis, we do not find that He gave them any commission to teach in the synagogues, as He was Himself accustomed to do. St Paul's case was different, as he was a Rabbi (Cp. *e.g.* Acts xiii. 5, 14, 15). Jesus always appealed to the written law (including the Psalms and Prophets) as a final authority ("the Scripture cannot be broken"—John x. 35); and fulfilled "all righteousness," as became one "made under the law" (Matt. iii. 15; Gal. iv. 4). But He quoted Scripture as having only a co-ordinate authority with his own word. His "Verily I say unto you" took the place of the old prophetic, "Thus saith the Lord." The position He assumed was that of supreme authority, immediately representing the sovereignty of God. He came, not like John the Baptist, to announce the kingdom of Heaven, but to found it, and to lay down its eternal laws.

From this brief view of the general character of our Lord's ministry, in relation to the Jewish rulers and to the mass of the nation, we can understand that Jerusalem would not be a suitable place for its exercise, except at the great yearly festivals. It is, therefore, likely that, having signalized the public opening of His ministry by the cleansing of the Temple, He did not prolong His stay in Jerusalem beyond the Passover Week. During this time He wrought some miracles, particulars of which are not recorded, but which led many to believe in Him, though the faith founded only on this external evidence was neither deep nor lasting (John ii. 23-25). In consequence of these miracles, He was visited by night by the distinguished Rabbi Nicodemus, whose faith, timidly concealed during the lifetime of Jesus, was nobly avowed after His death (John iii. 1-21; vii. 50; xix. 39). Shortly afterwards Jesus withdrew from the city, and began to preach and baptize in "the land of Judæa," in what locality we are not told; probably, like John, on the banks of Jordan (John iii. 22-36).

In attempting to determine the duration of this first ministry of our Lord in Judæa, we come on another controverted point. The question turns partly, though by no means wholly, on the interpretation of the words in John iv. 35 : "*Say not ye, There are yet four months, and then cometh harvest?*" Some (as Lightfoot, Robinson, Wieseler) take these words as supplying a literal note of time; and infer that our Lord's journey through Samaria took place about the beginning of December. Others (as Greswell, Alford) hold that the phrase, "*Say not ye*," implies a proverbial expression—"Four months, and then harvest;" that is, "You cannot have harvest in seed-time." Our Saviour's meaning, on this interpretation, is not that it was winter when He spoke, but that the proverbial four months had expired, and the fields were "white already to harvest." The literal harvest was the type of the spiritual harvest, of which the disciples themselves were the first-fruits, and which soon they were to toil in gathering in. According to the first view, Jesus spent eight months or more in Judæa. According to the second view, the time so spent, including the week at Jerusalem, was but about six weeks; and Pentecost (May 30) was at hand when Jesus left Judæa for Galilee.

It appears on the face of it in the highest degree improbable that our Lord should have spent three-fourths of the first year of His public ministry in Judæa without any record being preserved in any Gospel, beyond the brief statements that He tarried with His disciples in the land of Judæa, baptizing (by their ministry), and that the Pharisees heard that He was making more numerous disciples than John (John iii. 22; iv. 1-3). The "hill country" of Judæa, where the towns and villages were perched on the hill-tops, separated by steep, narrow valleys, was eminently unsuited to be the scene of such a ministry. And if, as seems likely, we are to understand that during this time our Lord was preaching, and gathering disciples in the valley of Jordan, even if He wrought no miracle, it is inconceivable that His fame should not in so long a time as eight months have filled all Palestine, attracting multitudes from Galilee and other regions. Instead of this, we find St. Matthew connecting the beginning of our Lord's public ministry and the rapid spread of His fame with His return to Galilee. This is intelligible, if He had been teaching publicly for some six weeks;

but not if He had been making more disciples than John during eight months. The narratives of St. Mark and St. Luke convey the same impression (Mark i. 14, 28; Luke iv. 14; comp. with Matt. iv. 17, 24). This impression is strongly confirmed by St. John's statement that "When He was come into Galilee, the Galilæans received Him, having seen all the things that He did at Jerusalem at the feast : for they also went unto the feast" (John iv. 45). By "the feast" is plainly meant the Passover spoken of in chap. ii. The reference is clear, if only a few weeks had elapsed, and no other feast had intervened. But if during eight months or more, including the feasts of Pentecost and Tabernacles, Jesus had been preaching and making disciples on the banks of Jordan, the statement would be inappropriate and inexplicable.

It is a further confirmation of this view, that Simon Peter, his brother, and their partners, James and John, on returning to Galilee, resumed their employment as fishermen. This was natural, if their absence had been but of a few weeks' duration; but the narratives in Matt. iv. 18–22, and Luke v. 1–11, would be scarcely intelligible, if during eight or nine months they had practically "left all" to follow Jesus.

The foregoing facts afford solid grounds for the conclusion that our Lord's EARLY JUDÆAN MINISTRY was limited to a few weeks, and that the summer was not yet far advanced when (perhaps in the last week of May) He journeyed with His little band of disciples through Samaria and Galilee (John iv. 3, 4).

While Jesus tarried in Judæa, "John also was baptizing in Ænon near to Salim. . . . For John was not yet cast into prison" (John iii. 23, 24). It seems now placed beyond doubt that Ænon and Salim were in the north of Samaria, and not far from the southern border of Galilee. We have already seen that John's ministry was by no means confined to the place where he at first baptized (John x. 40). Bethabara (or Bethania) appears to have been a ford between Peræa and Galilee considerably further north. That Herod "did many things" in compliance with John's exhortations "and heard him gladly" (Mark vi. 20), implies that John visited the court of the Tetrarch. And he must have been within Herod's territory, either in Galilee or in Peræa (and must, therefore, have left Ænon), when the tyrant seized and imprisoned him in his impregnable castle of Machærus, near the Dead Sea (Matt. xiv. 3; Mark vi. 17. See Jos., *Ant.* xviii. 5 : 2).

Our Lord's return to Galilee, and the beginning of His public ministry there, are connected in the first two Gospels with the imprisonment of John (Matt. iv. 12; Mark i. 14). The omission by St. Luke of any corresponding note of time (iv. 14) may be explained from the fact that he has previously referred to John's imprisonment (iii. 19, 20). St. John, after noting that the Baptist was still teaching and baptizing (at Ænon), while Jesus taught and baptized in Judæa, makes the remarkable statement (iv. 1–3), " When therefore the Lord knew how the Pharisees had heard that Jesus made and baptized more disciples than John, . . . He left Judæa, and departed again into Galilee." What are we to understand by this, or to infer from it? Very commonly it has been understood to imply, that our Lord's transference of His ministry from Judæa to Galilee, was in the nature of a retreat, or withdrawal for safety's sake from the hostility of the Pharisees. This view (how weighty or numerous soever the authorities which may be cited in its favour) appears to me a most serious and misleading misapprehension; and for these reasons :—

First. Because as yet there was no open breach between our Lord and the Pharisees. The first occasion of open hostility occurred at His next visit to Jerusalem, as recorded in John v. 1, 16, 18.

Secondly. It is dishonourable to Christ to ascribe to Him a timid care for personal safety, which even an apostle would have despised (comp. Luke xiii. 31–33; Acts xxi. 13). When the hostility of the Pharisees in league with the Sadducees had reached its height, two years and a half later, Jesus "steadfastly set His face to go to Jerusalem" (Luke ix. 51. Comp. John vii. 14, 25, 26; xi. 8, 9).[1]

Thirdly. If our Lord had wished to avoid danger, the only rational course would have been to refrain from public teaching altogether.

Fourthly. If our Lord's object was (as Lightfoot suggests) "that He might be more remote from that kind of thunderbolt that St. John had been struck with," He certainly would not have gone straight into the territory of Herod; not to seek "safe retirement" among the hills of Galilee, but to enter on a life of incessant public labour among the populous cities and thick-planted villages which bordered the Lake of Tiberias.

Galilee, with its swarming population, its green and wooded hills (so unlike the rugged and desolate mountains of the Judæan wilderness), and its lake, not, as now, a lonely waste of waters, but alive with sails and oars of fishing-craft and market-boats, presented incomparably the most suitable scene for the public ministry of Jesus. The Galilæans, hardy, brave, industrious, unpolished in speech, despised by the Jews of Jerusalem as rude and ignorant of the law, troubled themselves little, we may well suppose, in their turn, with the inane refinements and intoler-

[1] The brief suspension of public ministry noticed in John xi. 54 was of a totally different character: an interval of quiet private converse with His disciples; perhaps also of needful rest, bodily and mental, as well as solemn preparation for the tremendous closing conflict then near at hand.

able littleness of Rabbinical tradition. And, in spite of that spiritual dulness which Christ bewailed and rebuked (John iv. 48; Matt. xiii. 13–15; xi. 20), the hearts of these "lost sheep of the house of Israel" warmed towards the Teacher whose own loving heart yearned over them, who cared for their bodily as well as for their spiritual misery, who clothed Divine truth in homely guise, that it might "enter in at lowly doors," and bade the weary-hearted come to Him and find rest to their souls. The people of whom such "unlearned and ignorant men" as Peter and John were specimens, could have been no despicable people. Nor are we warranted in assuming that the associations of thirty years, and the ties of home and kindred, were treated by Christ with indifference, and allowed no share in determining the scene of His first public labours.

Instead, therefore, of explaining the return from Judæa to Galilee as a defeat or a retreat, we must rather regard it as an advance, and as the most natural and appropriate course for Jesus to adopt. If anything needs explaining, it is rather that He should have delayed His return to Galilee even for those few weeks during which He "tarried with His disciples" in the land of Judæa. This explanation, if I mistake not, is to be found in the fact, that John was still at this time carrying on his ministry close to the Galilæan border. Until his commission to "make ready a people prepared for the Lord" (Luke i. 17) had run out, the Lord Jesus wisely as well as generously refrained from appearing to supersede or rival him. He therefore confined Himself to the region which John had at first occupied, and had now quitted. We have thus the key to John iv. 1–3, which on this view refers not to any timid fear of the Pharisees, but to the fact (explained and illustrated by John iii. 25–30) that since by this time the fame of Jesus was known in Jerusalem to be eclipsing that of John, no practical end would have been served by any longer refraining from exercising His ministry in Galilee. John's noble words concerning the Bridegroom and the friend of the Bridegroom showed, that in the fading of his own light before the rising splendour of this greater Light, he recognized no failure or disappointment, but the fulfilment of his own witness, and the proof of the success of his mission.

That the imprisonment of John should have exactly coincided in time with the beginning of the Galilæan ministry of Christ, was an indication that his great work of preparing the way of the Lord was now accomplished. As its commencement and course were Divinely commissioned, so its close was Divinely ordered. St. Matthew tells us (iv. 12) that "Jesus had heard that John was cast into prison." Jesus, therefore, without further delay, "returned in the power of the Spirit into GALILEE" (Luke iv. 14). "And He must needs go through SAMARIA" (John iv. 4; that is to say, the *province* of Samaria, not the city), unless He preferred the circuitous route, beyond Jordan. It is asserted that Jews often took that route, to avoid Samaria; but Josephus tells us that, "it was customary for those Galilæans who went up to the Holy City at the festivals, to journey through the country of Samaria" (*Ant.* xx. 6 : 1); and he reckons it a three days' journey by this route from Galilee to Jerusalem (*Life*, § 52). Our Lord's two days' sojourn at Sychar, however, was not only a startling departure from Jewish customs, but a gracious exception to the rule which He laid down for Himself as well as for His disciples, to confine His ministry to Israel (Matt. xv. 24; x. 5, 6). The faith of these despised Samaritans was in striking contrast with the unbelief of Israel, especially as our Lord does not appear to have wrought any miracle among them. The field was "white to the harvest," and needed but to thrust in the sickle. It is interesting to connect with the welcome given to Christ by these strangers the ministry of Philip recorded in Acts viii. 5–8. (John iv. 1–44.)

The Galilæans, St. John tells us (iv. 45), readily welcomed Jesus, on account of the miracles which they had witnessed during the Passover Week at Jerusalem. Cana, where His first miracle had been wrought, was now the scene of a yet more wonderful display of Divine power, the healing of a nobleman's son, who was lying sick many miles away, at Capernaum (John iv. 46–54). Cana was not far from NAZARETH, and it is possible that Jesus may have paid private visits to His mother in the old home, which it did not belong to the Gospel history to record. But that He visited Capernaum, and wrought miracles there previous to the visit described by St. Luke (iv. 16–31), is clear from that very narrative (verse 23: "Whatsoever we have heard done in Capernaum," etc.; comp. verses 14, 15). At the same time the impression naturally conveyed is, that this visit belongs to an early period in the Galilæan ministry. Every consideration points to this as probable; and no solid reason can be advanced for the view maintained by many excellent writers, that in consequence of the murderous violence of the Nazarenes, our Lord never revisited Nazareth; and that this occasion must, therefore, be identified with that visit to "His own country" recorded in the first and second Gospels, when "He could there do no mighty work," and "marvelled because of their unbelief" (Matt. xiii. 53–58; Mark vi. 1–6). It is true that, had our Lord refrained from revisiting Nazareth, His townsmen would have been justly punished. Except that fatal death-shout of the Jewish people, "Crucify Him! His blood be on us and on our children!" no more astounding or melancholy words are on record than those which tell us how the men among whom the Son of Mary had lived for thirty years "were filled with wrath, and rose up, and thrust Him out of the city, and led Him unto the brow of the hill whereon their city was built, that they might cast Him down headlong." But surely He who was meek and lowly in heart, and who said even of blood-guilty Jerusalem, "How often would I have gathered thy children!" would not be deterred even by this outburst of insane pride and blind unbelief from revisiting, at least once more, the synagogue in which He had been wont in years past to take His turn among the Scripture readers, and according to His old neighbours one more proffer of grace. Their unbelief was none the less to be "marvelled at" because of its stubborn impenitence.

It has been sometimes said that Jesus did not "assume the title of MESSIAH." The statement is, perhaps, not very intelligible. He came not to fill an office and accept a title already in existence, but to do the work and BE the Person foreshadowed by that prophetic title of "the Anointed One." When men saw and heard Him they asked, "Is not this the Christ?" or exclaimed, "Thou art the Christ, the Son of the living God!" But, though no formal assumption of Messiahship was either requisite or possible, Jesus explicitly avowed at the very outset of His ministry that He was the predicted Messiah; as for example, to the Samaritan woman in wayside talk. (John iv. 26), and in public teaching at Nazareth, when He declared the prediction in Isaiah lxi. 1 to be fulfilled in Himself.

"From that time JESUS BEGAN TO PREACH, and to say, Repent: for the kingdom of heaven is at hand" (Matt. iv. 17).[1] To let all men understand that, great and vital as was the difference soon to be unfolded

[1] The expression in verse 13, "leaving Nazareth," need not be understood, in so terse a writer, to imply any renewed residence there, but may simply refer to the preceding thirty years.

between the ministry of the forerunner of Christ and that of Christ Himself, they were not discordant, but in truest harmony, the keynote of the early preaching of Jesus was an exact echo of that of the Baptist (comp. Mark. i. 14, 15). He took up the preaching of the Glad Tidings at the precise point where John had laid it down. But though the keynote was the same, that was but the prelude to a strain such as human ears never heard before. "Never man spake like this Man." Instead of a "voice crying in the wilderness," it was a voice in men's homes and hearts. Instead of a stern Elijah laying the axe to the root of the tree, it was the Good Shepherd seeking the lost sheep; the Sower going forth to sow; the Friend of sinners, who while He spoke of the living water and bread of life, fed the hunger of men's bodies, lifted off their burdens of sickness and infirmity, and wiped the tears of bereavement from their eyes. John's word had addressed the conscience, backing up its appeal with the terrors of judgment, yet also pointing to the Lamb of God who should bear away the sin of the world. Christ's word addressed the heart, the intellect, the whole spiritual nature. It joined with the call to repentance the assurance of full forgiveness, and the promise of the gift of God's Spirit to inspire within the soul a new life and fill the heart with comfort, peace, and rest. Those who had rejected John's ministry—the official lights and leaders of Israel—likewise rejected Christ; though on precisely contrary pretexts (Luke vii. 29–35). But the "publicans and sinners," as they had accepted John's baptism and confessed the justice of his scathing rebukes, crowded to the ministry of Jesus, as though they would take the kingdom of heaven by violence. (Matt. iv. 12–17; cf. xi. 12–14; Mark i. 14, 15; Luke iv. 14, 15.)

The first recorded occurrence in the Galilæan ministry is commonly spoken of as "THE CALL" OF THE FOUR DISCIPLES, Simon and Andrew, James and John, by the Lake of Galilee (Matt. iv. 18-22; Mark i. 16-20). This occasion is by many writers (including Calvin, Lightfoot, and Robinson) identified with that described in Luke v. 1-11. But *all the circumstances are irreconcilably different.* If the two accounts refer to the same occasion, a very large margin must be allowed for inaccuracy in the Evangelists. It is not a question of inspired infallibility, but of the accuracy without which no witness is trustworthy. In the narrative of Matthew and Mark, Jesus is walking by the lake; in that of Luke He has been sitting for a considerable time in Simon's boat, preaching to the crowd on the shore. In the former account both boats are afloat; Simon and Andrew are in the act of fishing; James and John are mending their dry nets, *preparatory* to fishing. In the latter account, both boats are drawn ashore; the fishermen have left them, and are washing their wet, soiled nets, *after* fishing all night.[1] In the one case, the four simply obey the call of Jesus, addressed to them from the shore, and leave their boats in charge of Zebedee and the hired helpers. In the other, after Simon's net (let down at Christ's command) has brought in a draught of fishes with which both boats are laden to the water's edge, they bring the boats to shore and follow Jesus, leaving their newly-gotten and surprising wealth to their companions as a compensation (we may suppose) for the withdrawal of their services. It seems scarcely possible that two narratives, so discrepant, should have been supposed to represent the same occurrence, but for a certain stiff, preconceived notion that there must have been an occasion, and but one, on which each disciple received a formal "call" to forsake secular life and attach himself to the person of Jesus. Such a

---

[1] If they were mending them they could not want washing, and if they were washing them they could not be mending them. Greswell has forcibly pointed out the difference of the accounts (*Dissertations*, vol. ii. Diss. ix.).

notion is quite inconsistent with the fact that at least three of the four here named had become disciples before Jesus returned to Galilee (John i. 35–42); and with the further fact that, when Jesus selected twelve out of the multitude of His disciples to be His constant attendants except when sent out as missionaries, their appointment or ordination was formally made with great solemnity, and is expressly recorded (Mark iii. 13-15). The multitude of His disciples received no personal call (John iv. 1, 2), and some, at least, who had received such a call disobeyed it (Luke ix. 59; Mark x. 21, 22). Not by a momentary word of command, or by a miraculous constraint, but gradually, by the irresistible spell of growing knowledge and affection, were the disciples of Jesus won to leave all and follow Him.

CAPERNAUM henceforth became, we cannot say the *home* of Him who "had not where to lay His head," but the head-quarters whence He started on His missionary tours, and to which He returned. (See Matt. iv. 13; Luke iv. 31, ix. 58.) We find no indication that His mother and brethren ceased to reside at Nazareth, though it might be imagined that, after the outrage recorded by St. Luke (iv. 28, 29), they would feel disposed to quit it. It is, at all events, evident from Mark iii. 21, 31, that His movements were so entirely independent of theirs as to be known to them only by public report. "For neither did His brethren believe on Him" (John vii. 5). "Peter's house" ("the house of Simon and Andrew") is spoken of as being in Capernaum (Matt. viii. 5, 14; Mark i. 21, 29), though Andrew and Peter are stated to have belonged to Bethsaida (John i. 44). We may infer that the brothers had removed to Capernaum, or else that the house thus spoken of was in reality the house of the parents of Peter's wife. And it would seem to have been this house which afforded Jesus a lodging in Capernaum—a hospitality munificently rewarded by the HEALING OF PETER'S MOTHER-IN-LAW. (Comp. Matt. xvii. 24, 25.)

The Sabbath on which this miracle was wrought, impressed thus ineffaceably on the mind of the Apostle Peter, is selected in the three synoptic Gospels as a specimen of our Lord's work at this stage of His ministry.

At the morning service in the Synagogue the Lord "healed ONE POSSESSED WITH A DEMON" (Mark i. 21–28; Luke iv. 31–37). At sunset, when the Sabbath ended, and it was lawful to carry the sick, "all the city was gathered together at the door" of the house where Jesus was; *i.e.*, at the outer gate of the court or yard. None departed unblessed. "He cast out the spirits with His word, and healed all that were sick;" thus affording, by His compassionate sympathy, as well as healing power, a glorious fulfilment of the prophetic word—" Himself took our infirmities, and bare our sicknesses." (Isa. liii. 4; Matt. viii. 14–17; Mark i. 29–34; Luke iv. 38–41.)

In St. Matthew's narrative two miracles are related, previous to the account of this Sabbath, which belong to a later period; but his object (in chaps. viii., ix.) is not to narrate events in order of time, but to place alongside of the specimen of Christ's teaching furnished in the "Sermon on the Mount" a series of miracles illustrating the brief summary of our Lord's labours at this period of His ministry given in chap. ix. 35, and chap. iv. 23–25.

Next morning (the first day of the week), "rising up a great while before day," Jesus sought the preparation of solitary prayer before setting forth on a mission tour in Galilee. Peter and some other of His disciples attended Him. (Mark i. 35–39; Luke iv. 42–44.) Teaching in the Synagogue is mentioned as a special feature at this time of His ministry. Everywhere the position of a prophet was conceded to Him, and the "authority" with which He taught, presenting a strong contrast with the perpetual appeal of the rabbinical teachers to oral tradition and the decisions of "the sages," impressed the multitude not less than His miracles. (Matt. vii. 28, 29. Compare, in reference to the closing months of His ministry, John vii. 40–46.)

Attempts have been made, with much care and study, to discriminate our Lord's missionary journeys as the " first circuit of Galilee," " second circuit," and the like; but such attempts appear to have no solid foundation in the Gospel narrative, and serve no useful purpose. The divinely-drawn picture is all the more impressive from the details not being over-sharply defined. The patient, loving labour of many weeks, or perhaps months, is summed up in the brief record that Jesus "preached in their Synagogues THROUGHOUT ALL GALILEE, and cast out devils" (Mark i. 39; Luke iv. 44). During these missionary tours Jesus may, probably, have repeatedly returned to Capernaum, and sojourned in "the house of Simon and Andrew." There is no reason to think that the future apostles were, as yet, His constant attendants. The narrative in Luke v. 1–11 seems to prove the contrary. The first effect of the amazing miracle there recorded was to arouse in Simon's mind a poignant sense of his sinfulness and unworthiness to be accounted a friend of Jesus. The gracious words of Jesus banished his fears; and as no miracle could have been so fitted to impress the minds of fishermen, so none could have supplied stronger encouragement to trust Jesus absolutely (the chief lesson of discipleship), and to forsake all at His bidding and for His sake.

To some time during the summer or early autumn of this year (A.D. 27), either between harvest and vintage, or between vintage and seed-time, when congregations could most easily be gathered in the open air, we may assign the "SERMON ON THE MOUNT." Is it really a *sermon*—a discourse delivered at one time to one company of hearers? Or is it a compilation of sayings uttered on various occasions? It is quite in accordance with the general plan and aim of St. Matthew's Gospel, that he should give a comprehensive specimen of our Lord's teaching at this stage of His ministry. Nevertheless, the impression which the reader naturally receives from chapters v.-vii. of St. Matthew's Gospel is, that they contain a report of a single discourse. The report may be condensed, possibly even supplemented from other discourses; but it is no mere compilation of fragments, but a connected and majestic whole. In the tone of unlimited authority, the Master depicts the character of His true disciples, and their mission as the "salt" and "light" of human society; exemplifies (in strong contrast with the notions of the "Scribes and Pharisees") the "righteousness"—that is, both morality and religion—required of them; and warns His hearers that to reject Him, or be rejected by Him, implies exclusion from God's kingdom, and that to hear His word without obeying it is to build on the sand.

The HEALING OF A LEPER, placed in the first Gospel immediately after the Sermon on the Mount (Matt. viii. 2-4), and more fully narrated in the second and third Gospels (Mark i. 40-45; Luke v. 12-15), marks a stage of our Lord's ministry when He found it needful to lay restraint on the publication of His miraculous cures. This has been attributed (like His removal from Judæa to Galilee) to caution and timidity. The objections to all such views have been already set forth. In some instances, privacy was important for the sake of the persons themselves who were healed (Jairus' daughter, for example, Mark v. 43); but, in general, we need seek no further explanation than that furnished by the Evangelist, to wit, that our Lord's movements were impeded, and His great work of teaching hindered, by the multitude who crowded to be healed. (Mark i. 45; iii. 20; Luke v. 15. Cf. p. 88.)

The last recorded events which we can assign to these first twelve months of Christ's ministry, are the miracle of healing "ONE SICK OF THE PALSY," at Capernaum, and the CALL OF MATTHEW, or Levi (Matt. ix. 2-8, 9; Mark ii. 1-12, 13, 14; Luke v. 17-26, 27, 28). On the first of these occasions we are told that "there were Pharisees and doctors of the law sitting by, who were come out of every town of Galilee, and Judæa, and Jerusalem." The crowd was so great, that the bearers of the sick man, unable to force an entrance into the courtyard of the house where Jesus was preaching, entered that of a neighbouring house, made their way up the outside staircase to the flat roof, and lowered their burden to the feet of Jesus "*through* the tiling." We are probably to understand that our Lord was seated in a gallery or balcony, into which the principal room of the house opened, so that He could be heard both by those around and behind Him, and by the crowd in the courtyard; and that it was the roof of this gallery which was broken up—a matter of no great labour or serious damage.

It is reasonable to suppose that Matthew was no stranger to Jesus, when at those startling but heart-stirring words, "*Follow me*," "he left all, rose up, and followed Him." If we are right in our date for the Sermon on the Mount, we must suppose that Matthew had already been an attentive hearer of the Master's word, and a disciple in heart, though he had not till now seen it his duty to give up his worldly calling. The notion that our Saviour would have suddenly addressed such a command to one in whom He discerned no inward preparation to obey it, is inconsistent with His solemn warnings against hasty, thoughtless discipleship (Luke xiv. 25-33; ix. 57, 58).

The call of Matthew (or Levi) is in all these

Gospels connected with the feast at his house, when, to the amazement and indignation of the Pharisees, Jesus did not scruple to sit at table " with publicans and sinners." The connection is natural, almost necessary, but it is the connection of events, not of time. This is clear, if we compare the three Gospels. For the application of Jairus, which followed close upon the feast (Matt. ix. 10–18), was subsequent to the visit to Gadara, or Gerasa (Mark v. 21, 22; Luke viii. 40, 41); and that visit is clearly shown, by the second and third Gospels, to have been subsequent to the choice of the Twelve, and to the walk through the cornfields; in other words, to belong to the *second summer* of Christ's ministry (A.D. 28). An interval of time, therefore, more or less considerable, separated the call of Matthew from the farewell feast (as we may suppose it to have been) to which he invited his brother publicans.

This first twelvemonth of our Lord's ministry was its most peaceful, and, to human judgment, prosperous and hopeful period. The unbelief and murderous rage of the Nazarenes stands out in harsh, threatening contrast with its general tenor. The fame of the new Prophet " went throughout all Syria," casting into the shade the ministry of His great forerunner; for " John did no miracle, but all things that John spake of this man were true " (John x. 41). Multitudes believed. Rabbis from Jerusalem sat among Christ's hearers and witnessed His miracles; though some of them were indignant at His claims, and justified their scepticism by ascribing His miracles to the power of Satan (Mark ii. 6, 7; iii. 22). But their hostility had not openly burst forth. The times seem bright with promise. Perhaps to no eye but His were the gathering clouds visible which, in that peaceful morning of His ministry, among the green hills of Galilee, were already brewing the tempest amidst which that ministry was to close.

FIRST YEAR OF MINISTRY.

The Miracles of our Saviour are classified by Dr. Westcott (in his excellent little book, *Characteristics of the Gospel Miracles*) as follows :
I. MIRACLES ON NATURE.
 i. Miracles of Power. 1. Water made wine. 2. Bread multiplied (twice). 3. Walking on the sea.
 ii. Miracles of Providence. 1. Draught of fishes (twice). 2. Tempest stilled. 3. Money in fish's mouth. 4. Fig tree withered.
II. MIRACLES ON MAN.
 i. Miracles of Personal Faith. 1. Two blind men (Matt. ix.). 2. Bartimæus. 3. The leper. 4. Ten lepers. 5. Woman in crowd.
 ii. Miracles of Intercession. 1. Blind man (Mark viii.). 2. Deaf and dumb man (Mark vii.). 3. Nobleman's son. 4. Centurion's servant. 5. Paralytic.
 iii. Miracles of Love. 1. Man born blind. 2. Peter's mother-in-law. 3. Man with dropsy. 4. Withered arm. 5. Impotent man. 6. Woman with spirit of infirmity. 7. Dead raised: (*a*) from the sick bed ; (*b*) from the bier ; (*c*) from the grave. [Add 8, Malchus' ear healed.]
III. MIRACLES ON THE SPIRIT-WORLD.
 i. Miracles of Intercession. 1. Dumb demoniac (Matt. ix.). 2. Blind and dumb demoniac (Matt. xii.). 3. Syro-Phœnician's daughter. 4. Boy brought by his father.
 ii. Miracles of Antagonism. 1. The demoniac in synagogue. 2. Legion of demons.

To this list we may add, under Class I., *Obscure Miracles:* (1) The vanishing of our Saviour's person (thrice, Luke iv. 30 ; xxiv. 51 ; John viii. 59) ; (2) His appearance in the midst of the disciples when the doors were shut (twice, John xx. 19, 26). With Class II. we may connect the exercise of superhuman control over men: (1) in the cleansing of the Temple (twice) ; (2) in the Garden of Gethsemane (John xviii. 6). In John vi. 21, it is open to question whether a miracle is intended. The two greatest miracles, the RESURRECTION and the ASCENSION, stand alone, and are not included in the foregoing classification.

On the unreasonable modern prejudice against miracles, see Dr. H. R. Reynolds's *John the Baptist*, pp. 13-16 : *The Basis of Faith*, Lec. vi., sec. 4, pp. 254-272 (2nd Ed.).

SECTION II.

SECOND YEAR OF MINISTRY.

FROM PASSOVER A.D. 28 TO PASSOVER A.D. 29.
(A.U.C. 781, 782.)

IF we would trace a clear outline of our Saviour's life and ministry, we must be content with an outline, and must resist the temptation to labour after a fulness and exactitude for which the Gospels do not supply the materials. We must free ourselves from the notion that the object of the Gospels bound the writers to strict chronological order, so that in relating events in a different sequence they are guilty of misplacing them, or, if they pass them by in silence, are mutilating history. The object of the Gospels is neither historical nor biographical, but religious. "These are written," says St. John, "that ye might believe that JESUS is the Christ, the Son of God, and that, believing, ye might have life through His name." The systematic unity and simplicity of plan (almost resembling the unity of an epic poem) which distinguish the fourth Gospel from the others, render it natural—almost necessary—for St. John to adhere to chronological order in what he narrates; but he passes by in absolute silence the largest portion of our Saviour's life, including nearly all, except the closing scenes, which the former Gospels had recorded. With the Evangelist, as with the preacher, the object is to furnish, not a manual of facts and dates, but a picture which shall live in the memory and heart. It is, therefore, a pedantic and inappreciative, not to say ignorant, criticism which censures or slights the Gospels as "fragmentary." That they leave unnoticed large spaces of our Saviour's ministry, as well as nearly thirty years of His life, is in perfect harmony with their practical object, and with the purpose of the inspiring Spirit, who was preparing (unknown to the writers) not a text-book of scientific history, but a practical guide to faith, to be studied in all languages to the end of time.

"After this there was a feast of the Jews; and JESUS WENT UP TO JERUSALEM" (John v. 1). What feast this was is a much-debated and important question, the answer to which has been regarded as furnishing the key to the chronology of the Gospel narrative. To some extent it does so, for, if this feast was a Passover, then we have four Passovers distinctly noted in St. John's Gospel (ii. 13; v. 1; vi. 4; xi. 55), necessarily implying a duration of three years for our Lord's ministry. The converse, however, is not true. If it was *not* a Passover, it does not follow that that ministry lasted less than three years. If it was not the Passover, it does not in fact greatly matter to the Gospel chronology what feast it was. For, in addition to the separate evidence on which we assign the cleansing of the Temple to A.D. 27, and the Crucifixion to A.D. 30, we have independent proof from the synoptic Gospels of *the occurrence of a Passover* between that which preceded the Galilæan ministry and that which was approaching (John vi. 4), when our Lord fed the five thousand in the wilderness. This proof consists in the narrative of the walk through the cornfields on the Sabbath, when the disciples offended the Pharisees by plucking the ripe ears of corn and rubbing them out in their hands. This could not have happened before a Passover, not only because the corn would not be ripe, but because the disciples would not have dared to gather it until after the sacred sheaf of firstfruits had been offered in the Temple. Moreover, the difficult phrase in Luke vi. 1 (literally, "the second-first Sabbath"), whatever be its precise meaning, points, it can hardly be doubted, to a Passover.[1] But we are forbidden by Matt. xii. 1 to identify the Passover thus indicated with that at the beginning of our Lord's ministry (John ii. 13). And unless we surrender the task of framing any connected view of the Gospel history, we are equally forbidden by the three synoptic narratives to identify it with that Passover (John vi. 4) which followed the death of John the Baptist, the return of the Twelve, and the feeding of the five thousand.

It is of course conceivable that the feast mentioned in John v. 1 may have been the Feast of Tabernacles (A.D. 27). But no reason can be given for such a supposition. In the absence of contrary evidence, we may assume that our Lord would adhere to the custom in which He had been trained from childhood of going up "to Jerusalem every year at the Feast of the Passover" (Luke ii. 41). The events which happened at the feast amply account for His absenting Himself from Jerusalem for a period of eighteen months, until the Feast of Tabernacles (A.D. 29), six months before His death.

This SECOND VISIT TO JERUSALEM, which on the foregoing grounds we assign to the Passover of A.D. 28, was a memorable crisis in the life and ministry of our Lord, a fatal turning-point in the history of the Jewish nation. The bigotry, jealousy, and wounded pride of the Jewish rulers now broke out into open hostility, and the purpose was formed, and even (it would seem) avowed, to put Jesus to death. The immediate occasion of this open breach was the HEALING ON THE SABBATH DAY OF AN INFIRM MAN, incurably diseased for thirty-eight years, who was

---

[1] The simplest explanation seems to be, that it means "the first Sabbath of the second month"—namely, Zif— when wheat was ripe. Wieseler's explanation, that it means the first Sabbath of the second year after a Sabbatic year is untenable, because the Sabbatic year began in autumn.

seeking relief from the medicinal virtue of the Pool of Bethesda.[1] Even had he been aware of the power of Jesus, he might not have dared to ask a cure on the Sabbath. Our Lord's ordinary rule was to put forth His healing power in answer to the prayer of faith; but on this occasion He uttered unsolicited the command, "Rise, take up thy bed and walk." Conscious (perhaps for the first time) of the strange sensation of bodily vigour, the man sprang to his feet, and did not hesitate to obey the command by rolling up his mat-bed and carrying it away. So manifest a breach of the received interpretation of the law of the Sabbath (comp. Jer. xvii. 21; Neh. xiii. 15, 19), brought on him instant notice and rebuke. The man sheltered himself under the authority of his unknown Healer. On learning subsequently that it was Jesus who had thus "broken the Sabbath," the wrath of the Jewish rulers was turned full upon Him. It is supposed (by Lightfoot and others) that Jesus was summoned before the Sanhedrin; but St. John's narrative leaves it uncertain whether they ventured to call Him before them, or merely sent a deputation to remonstrate with Him. Jesus, instead of bowing to the storm, assumed ground which in their eyes added crime to crime. He placed His own works of mercy on a moral level with the beneficent activity of the Creator, whereby the Sabbath is not profaned, but blest; at the same time claiming to be in some special sense the Son of God. "My Father," He said, "worketh hitherto, and I work." This reply aggravated the fury of the rulers, who now resolved on the death of Jesus. The discourse in which Christ then unfolded His claims (John v. 19–47) was one of the sublimest which ever fell even from His lips. He spoke with startling plainness, as One subject to the authority of no earthly tribunal, but Himself the Divinely-appointed Judge of men.

[1] See Conder's *Handbook to the Bible*, p. 357.

The awe inspired by the majesty of this discourse, and the heart-searching keenness of its rebukes and warnings, paralyzed for the time the murderous purpose of the Sanhedrin. Jesus left the Holy City, to return no more until that time (six months before His death) when " He steadfastly set His face to go to Jerusalem " (Luke ix. 51). But the determination to put Him to death was cherished with undying animosity, "because He not only had broken the Sabbath, but said also that God was His Father, making Himself equal with God" (John v. 18). A year and a half afterwards, the first of these charges was still fresh in men's memories. In John vii. 23 (where the translation should read, " because I made a man every whit whole on the Sabbath day ") the reference is evidently to this miracle. On the second charge Jesus was twice on the point of being stoned in the Temple (John viii. 59; x. 31-33); and this was the main accusation brought against Him before Pilate, although, in order to induce the Roman Governor to sentence Him to death, a further charge was preferred of sedition against the Imperial Government.

This question of the Sabbath (the importance of which, in Jewish eyes, it is impossible to exaggerate) was soon again raised under different circumstances. Some disciples of Jesus, walking with their Master through the cornfields ON THE SABBATH, PLUCKED EARS OF CORN, which they rubbed out and ate. The law expressly permitted passengers through cornfields to do this (Deut. xxiii. 25). But, according to the rabbinical rules, plucking the ears was reaping, and rubbing them out was threshing, involving a double breach of the Sabbath. The Lord defended "the guiltless" on two grounds. 1st, As warranted by Scripture examples and by the very intention of the Sabbath, in satisfying their hunger. 2nd, Because they were in the service of One " greater than the Temple," and " Lord even of the Sabbath day."

(Matt. xii. 1–8; Mark ii. 23–28; Luke vi. 1–5.) If the ripe corn was barley, the time indicated was April; if wheat, May or the close of April. In either case we must suppose the incident to have occurred after our Lord's return from Jerusalem to Galilee; which return is implied, though not expressly mentioned, by St. John (vi. 1).

Another Sabbath miracle seems to belong to this period, THE HEALING OF A WITHERED HAND in the Synagogue, probably at Capernaum. On this occasion our Lord, calling the sufferer to stand forth in the midst, appealed to the practice and conscience of the Pharisees themselves, in proof of the lawfulness of doing good on the Sabbath. Then amid their sullen silence, He simply bade the man stretch out his hand, "and it was restored whole like as the other." The Pharisees, the more enraged because here was undeniably no overt act of Sabbath-breaking, called to their aid "the Herodians" (comp. Matt. xxii. 16), and "took counsel" how they might destroy Him. These proud and bigoted pretenders to religious perfection—"the separated ones"—were willing to ally themselves not only with the worldly and time-serving adherents of the detested house of Herod, but with their hated opponents, the Sadducees (Matt. xvi. 1), to compass the destruction of Jesus, whom they were beginning to dread as much as to hate. (Matt. xii. 9–14; Mark iii. 1–6; Luke iv. 6–11.)

Jesus, aware of these plots, WITHDREW WITH HIS DISCIPLES to a quiet spot on the shores of the lake, far from towns and synagogues, and from the company of all save those who were drawn to Him by their desire to hear His word, or their need of His healing mercy. During the rainless months of summer, when harvest and the harvest feast (Pentecost) were past, and field-labour in great measure suspended, His growing fame attracted crowds from great distances. "A great multitude from Galilee followed Him, and from Judæa, and from Jerusalem, and from Idumæa, and from beyond Jordan (Peræa); and they about Tyre and Sidon, a great multitude, when they had heard what great things He did, came unto Him." (Matt. xii. 15-21; Mark iii. 7-12.) He repulsed no appeal to His pity, the promptness and human tenderness of which was the true image of Divine compassion. But His chief aim was to heal men's souls; and this crowd of applicants for mere bodily relief was a serious hindrance to His work as a teacher. Smaller gatherings of earnest hearers, giving opportunity for personal converse, were far more favourable to His main object of bringing the "lost sheep" home to God, than the excitement of worldly-minded crowds bent only on being spectators or subjects of miracles. Jesus therefore enjoined silence on those whom He healed. His glorious simplicity of aim and contempt for mere popularity and fame admirably fulfilled the ancient prophecy, Isaiah xlii. 1-4.

The Lord now took a step pregnant with the most important meaning and results. After a night spent in prayer among those mountain solitudes to which He loved to retreat for this purpose, He called around Him a large number of His professed disciples, from amongst whom "HE CHOSE TWELVE, whom also He named APOSTLES; that they should be with Him, and that He might send them forth to preach, and to have power to heal sicknesses, and to cast out devils." (Mark iii. 13-19; Luke vi. 12-16; comp. Matt. x. 2-4.) Descending with the Twelve and the rest of His disciples to some open level spot, where a vast concourse from all parts speedily gathered round Him, "to hear Him, and to be healed of their diseases" (Luke vi. 17-19), He pronounced a discourse, of which St. Luke gives a brief report, and which by many critics is identified with the Sermon on the Mount (Luke vi. 20-49). The choice and ordination of the twelve apostles, whose number evidently had reference

to that of the tribes of Israel, clearly indicated that
Jesus designed His own preaching to be but the commencement of a systematic and permanent mission
addressed in the first instance to the Jewish nation,
but eventually to the whole human race.[1] This
double purpose was clearly expressed in the solemn
charge which He addressed to the Twelve when,
some months later, He sent them forth on their first
missionary tour. (Comp. Luke xxiv. 47; Acts i. 8.)

With this solemn public avowal, at once to the
disciples and to the world, of plans and claims immeasurably transcending those of any former prophet,
teacher, or lawgiver; and with those indefatigable
labours which left neither leisure no privacy for a
quiet meal, St. Mark's narrative connects the ATTEMPT
OF THE UNBELIEVING KINDRED of Jesus to put Him
under restraint; "for they said, He is beside Himself" (Mark iii. 21). It is important to notice that
the latter part of verse 19—"And they went into a
house"—ought properly to be printed, not merely as
a separate verse, but (as in Scrivener's and Dean
Alford's texts, and in Mr. Darby's valuable *New
Translation*) as the beginning of a fresh paragraph.
St. Mark appears closely to connect with this attempt

[1] The Greek word *Apostolos* is used once in the *LXX.
Translation of the Old Testament* for one "sent" with a
message (1 Kings xiv 6). It appears, however, that "with
the Jews of the Christian era the word was in common use.
It was the title borne by those who were despatched from
the mother city by the rulers of the race on any foreign
mission, especially such as were charged with collecting the
tribute paid for the Temple service. After the destruction
of Jerusalem the 'Apostles' formed a sort of council about
the Jewish Patriarch, assisting him in his deliberations at
home, and executing his orders abroad." Thus, in selecting
this title for His ambassadors (2 Cor. v. 20), "our Lord was
not introducing a new term, but adopting one which from
its current usage would suggest to His hearers the idea of a
highly responsible mission" (*Bishop Lightfoot on Galatians*,
pp. 93, 94, Third Ed.).

the request of the mother and brethren of Jesus to see Him, when engaged in teaching (ver. 31–35). But St. Matthew (xiii. 1) places that incident on the same day with the teaching in parables, on the evening of which day (Mark iv. 35) our Lord crossed the lake. Some interval is necessarily implied in the words, "*When His friends heard.*" The connection is no doubt close and real; but it is that of the events themselves, not of mere time.

Upon our Lord's return to Capernaum—probably to Peter's house (Mark iii. 19; Luke vii. 1)—an urgent petition was presented to Him by the Jewish elders on behalf of a ROMAN CENTURION, whose servant, "who was dear unto him," was sick and ready to die. This remarkable intercession was due to the fact that this Gentile soldier had shown his zeal for true religion, and love for God's people, by building a synagogue. St. Luke describes with literal accuracy the form of the application by means first of the elders, then of a second deputation of friends. St. Matthew, in his brief, condensed style, says that the centurion "*came unto Him:*" not only on the familiar principle that "what one does by another one does one's self" (*qui facit per alium facit per se*; comp. Matt. xxvii. 26), but because this was the spiritual reality of the petition. The centurion came to Christ in the same sense as we come to Him in prayer. The name is left unrecorded of this pious Gentile, whose faith and humility won from the Lord one of the most emphatic eulogies He is ever recorded to have uttered. (Matt. viii. 5–13; Luke vii. 1–10.)

At Jerusalem, at the feast which we have seen reason to believe was the Passover (from which we reckon the second year of His public ministry), our Lord had declared that the Father would show Him "greater works" than the miracles of healing He had already performed, empowering Him even to raise the dead to life. The first recorded example of this is

narrated by St. Luke only—THE RAISING OF A DEAD
MAN, the only son of a widow, as the corpse was being
carried to burial. NAIN, the scene of this miracle
(where tombs cut in the rock are at this day the only
remains of the ancient "city") is an hour's ride from
the foot of Mount Tabor, and nearly twenty miles as
the crow flies (of course much further on foot) from
even the most southerly site assigned to Capernaum.
It has been questioned, therefore, whether it was
practicable for Jesus to make this long journey in a
single day. It is not quite certain that "the day
after" is the true reading: some manuscripts read
"afterwards." But if it be, our Lord, rising early
according to His custom, may have performed part of
the journey by water (sailing down, as Dr. Farrar
suggests, to the south end of the lake; or, as I would
rather suggest, to Magdala). Possibly St. Luke's
phrase may simply mean that the next day He set
forth on His way to the town of Nain. The fame of
this great miracle, proving that God had visited His
people and raised up a great prophet, spread throughout the land. (Luke vii. 11–17.)

Here follows in St. Luke's orderly narrative one of
the most touching and impressive incidents in the
whole course of our Saviour's ministry,—THE MESSAGE
SENT BY JOHN THE BAPTIST from his prison. Different
minds will probably always come to different conclusions on the much-debated question whether John
sent this message for his own satisfaction, or merely
for the sake of his disciples, that their faith might be
confirmed in the Messiah to whom he had borne witness. Calvin scouts the supposition that John's own
faith could have wavered or needed reinforcement as
"*valde absurdum.*" Stier and Alford argue forcibly
on the same side. It seems to me, however, that
their view is not merely inconsistent with the natural
impression vividly conveyed in both Gospels, but
leaves out of account the weakness of human nature

even in the strongest, as well as the peculiar severity of John's trial, and the probable effect both on body and mind of his prolonged incarceration in the dungeons of Machærus. Trained in the wild freedom of the desert, in the prime of manhood, accustomed since he received his Divine commission to the excitement of open-air preaching, and the sympathy of enthusiastic crowds, he was perhaps the one man of all men to whom the horrors of solitary imprisonment would be most intolerable. What more natural than that it should appear an inscrutable mystery, that Jesus, the Prophet whom even death obeyed, the Christ to whom he had borne witness, was leaving His faithful herald to languish, forgotten and unpitied in his cell? What wonder if he began to question whether even Jesus Himself were more than the forerunner of a yet greater Deliverer? The faith which trusts in the dark is far harder than the faith which believes when favoured with he full light of .nspiration.

Christ replied by making John's disciples eye-witnesses to miracles such as those the fame of which had penetrated his dungeon, and by a gracious word of encouragement tenderly conveying a no less gracious admonition—not to say reproof—to His sorely tried servant. When the messengers were departed Jesus pronounced a splendid eulogy on the imprisoned prophet. (Luke vii. 18-35; Matt. xi. 2-19.)

St. Matthew's narrative seems to place this incident after the sending forth of the Twelve; but this discrepancy is apparent only, not real. A new section of his Gospel begins with ch. xi. 2, including ch. xii. 1-8; and the chronological clue given in ch. xii. 1, if rigidly interpreted, would give even an earlier date than St. Luke's narrative. We may take it in a somewhat wide sense. Comp. ch. xi. 25.

Here St. Matthew's Gospel introduces Christ's severe DENUNCIATION OF THE IMPENITENT CITIES, in which so many of His miracles had been wrought; and that solemn THANKSGIVING TO HIS FATHER, which St. Luke introduces in connection with the mission and return of the seventy (Matt. xi. 20–27; Luke x. 13–15, 21, 22). If we were shut up to the belief that words like these could only have been uttered once, we could hardly hesitate to consider the place assigned to them by St. Luke as the true one; both because the sayings themselves appear appropriate to a late period of our Lord's ministry, and because St. Luke so circumstantially connects them with the sending forth and return of the seventy preachers. Calvin takes this view. If, on the other hand (with Greswell, Robinson, Stier, Alford), we consider St. Matthew's phraseology (verses 20, 25) too definite to permit the supposition that he here disregards the order of time, we must remember that no reason can be shown why our Lord should not have repeated such memorable sayings, if occasion demanded. Indeed, we have ample proof that such was His habit. St. Matthew alone records the gracious invitation which through so many ages has comforted innumerable labouring and heavy-laden hearts: "COME UNTO ME, ALL YE THAT LABOUR AND ARE HEAVY LADEN, AND I WILL GIVE YOU REST."

St. Luke alone relates how our Lord AT THE TABLE OF A PHARISEE, who entertained Him with scant courtesy, received the worship of "a woman in the city who was a sinner" and pronounced her sins forgiven (Luke vii. 36–50). The legend which identifies this unnamed penitent with Mary of Magdala rests on no shadow of foundation, and appears inconsistent with the mention of Mary as one of those who accompanied Jesus, and "ministered unto Him of their substance" (Luke viii. 1–3). Even recent writers have clung to it for the sake of the romance of poetry and painting which has gathered like a halo around it. But it is in the last degree improbable that our Lord would have admitted among His attendants one whose penitence, sincere as He knew it to be, had yet to be proved; or that matrons of rank and wealth would have accepted such an associate. Our Saviour's words of forgiveness were also words of farewell: not "COME, FOLLOW," but "GO IN PEACE." The legend perhaps arose from confounding this occurrence with the anointing at Bethany (John xii. 3).

A mass of unrecorded labour and benefaction is summed up in the brief statement that "He went throughout every city and village, preaching and shewing the glad tidings of the kingdom of God; and the Twelve were with Him" (Luke viii. 1). From this multitude of miracles, one is selected for record, —THE HEALING OF A BLIND AND DUMB DEMONIAC— not only on its own account, but as having given occasion to the blasphemies of the Scribes who came down from Jerusalem. Unable to deny the miracles of Jesus, they ascribed them to Satanic power. St. Mark omits this miracle, but agrees with St. Matthew in connecting with the discourse spoken on this occasion (apparently in the house in which the afflicted man had been brought to Jesus) the application of "HIS MOTHER AND HIS BRETHREN," who, "standing without, sent unto Him, calling Him," and our Saviour's memorable reply. (Matt. xii. 22–50; Mark iii. 22–35; Luke xi. 14–26; viii. 19–21.)

It was on this same day that Jesus went forth from the house to the lake side, and taking His seat, according to His custom (Luke v. 3; Mark iii. 9), in a fishing-boat, preached to the multitudes assembled on the sand. The season was not yet far enough advanced for these great open-air gatherings to be hindered by the autumn rains or by the toils of the field; but the time was at hand when the ploughman must yoke his oxen, and the sower go forth to sow. Neither the hostility of the Jewish rulers, nor the blasphemies of "the Scribes from Jerusalem," backed up by the perverse fancy of His kindred that Jesus had lost His reason, availed to check the popular enthusiasm. But in most it was enthusiasm only, not faith and penitence. The Son of Man had come not to draw crowds, but to save the lost. The cities poured forth their eager thousands, but "they repented not." Every village sent forth curious listeners and spectators, together with sick and suffering petitioners, but "hearing they heard, and did not understand, and seeing they saw, and did not perceive." The great Teacher therefore betook Himself to TEACHING IN PARABLES. If His "word" (as He called His doctrine) could not penetrate their dull minds, He would at least fix His *words* in their memory, to yield up in after days their hidden treasure of meaning. Partly to the multitude, partly to His disciples. He spoke the SEVEN PARABLES of the kingdom recorded by St. Matthew (xiii. 3-52), and ONE preserved in St. Mark's Gospel only (iv. 26-34); "but without a parable spake He not unto them." We are not to understand that our Lord had previously never used similitudes; for not only is it inconceivable that among Orientals a preacher should instruct his congregation, or a teacher his scholars, without making use of similes and allegories, but in the Sermon on the Mount we have the parable of the Two Builders, and the similitudes of the Salt, the Light, and the City (Matt. v. 13-16; vii. 24-27). But what seems to have surprised the disciples on this occasion was the Master's almost exclusive use of this form of teaching, and His keeping back the interpretation to be communicated to His disciples in private. St. Mark (iv. 33) alludes to "many such parables," which may have been spoken partly on this, partly on other occasions. (Matt. xiii. 1-52; Mark iv. 1-34; Luke viii. 4-18; xiii. 18-21.)

No day of human history, no words uttered in human ears, have impressed themselves more indelibly on human memory that the events and sayings of this one day in the life of Jesus. As evening drew

THE SOWER.

on He dismissed the multitude and returned to the house—presumably for the evening meal. He then "gave commandment" to cross the lake, and Himself led the way to the ship.[1]

A WOULD-BE FOLLOWER was checked by being told that although even the wild creatures had their dens and roosting-places, the Son of Man—the anointed King of mankind—was a houseless wanderer. May we gather from our Lord's words that the tenants of the house in which He had been entertained during the day were unable or unwilling to afford Him and His disciples a night's lodging, so that He was constrained to make the boat which had been His pulpit serve for His bed? Or did He hear in His spirit the cries of those wretched maniacs among the tombs on the farther shore, and hasten through the night and the storm to deliver them? Spent with the strain which such a day inflicted on both body and mind, Jesus found "where to lay His head" on the steersman's cushion, and slept calmly. One of those sudden squalls to which, like other mountain-girded lakes, the Sea of Galilee is subject, threatened to sink the boat; but still the Lord slept until the cries of the disciples awoke Him. Then with that authority which is Nature's supreme law, He QUELLED THE TEMPEST, rebuking His disciples for their lack of faith. (Matt. viii. 18–27; Mark iv. 35–41; Luke viii. 22–25).

Soon after daybreak, we may suppose, of that calm summer morning, was wrought the great act of mercy for which that strange night voyage had been under-

[1] St. Mark's phrase (iv. 36), "They took Him even as He was in the ship," must not be so pressed as to contradict St. Matthew's statement that the explanation of the parables was given *in the house* (xiii. 36). It must mean just *as He had been sitting* in the boat—the same boat, and with no preparation or provision. Regardless as our Lord might be of His own comfort, He would not, after a day spent in attendance upon Himself, have required His disciples to set forth supperless on their stormy night voyage.

taken—the healing of a fierce and dangerous maniac, possessed not with one, but with A LEGION OF DEMONS. (St. Matthew notes that he had a companion.) The various names by which the scene of this miracle is called in different manuscripts and versions—"the country of the Gadarenes," "Gergesenes," "Gerasenes," "Gazarenes,"—may be due, in part at least, to errors in copying. Gadara was far away; but it is conceivable that the term "land of Gadara" may have extended to the border of the lake. The simplest view, however, is that "Gerasa" and "Gergesa" are two forms of the same name (probably derived from the ancient Girgashites); and that Origen was well informed in stating that the site of the city—Gergesa—and the scene of the miracle were shown in his day. Dr. W. M. Thomson's identification with the modern Khersa or Gersa is at present doubtful.[1] The destruction of an enormous herd of swine, by permission (not command) of Jesus, was perhaps intended to attest the reality of the demoniac possession; perhaps also to punish the insult offered to the Mosaic law by the presence of these unclean animals in the Holy Land. Terrified at this portent, the inhabitants of the city offered perhaps the most foolish prayer on record, in compliance with which Jesus re-embarked and returned to "His own city." (Matt. viii. 18—ix. 1; Mark iv. 35—v. 21; Luke viii. 22–40.)

From the accounts in the second and third Gospels we might imagine that the application of the synagogue ruler JAIRUS was made as soon as Jesus reached the shore, where the people "were all waiting for Him." But St. Matthew expressly states (ix. 18) that

[1] See *The Land and the Book*, pp. 375-378. Dean Stanley thinks the site was farther north, at Wady Fik (*Sin. and Pal.*, p. 380). This city must not be confounded with Gerasa (Jerash, not named in the Bible), a city of Decapolis, the ruins of which have been judged superior to those of Palmyra. See *Cyclopædia Bib. Lit.*, vol. ii. p. 111.

Jairus presented his request whilst Jesus was uttering that discourse concerning the difference between John's disciples and His own, which arose out of the offence taken by the Pharisees at seeing Jesus and His disciples sitting at table with "many publicans and sinners." Here, therefore, we must place the FEAST IN MATTHEW'S HOUSE, which in all three Gospels is narrated in immediate connection with the call of Matthew or Levi: a striking and instructive instance of the manner in which the order of time is subordinated to that of subject. (Matt. ix. 10–17; Mark ii. 15–22; Luke v. 29–39.)

As the feast in Matthew's house was "a great reception" (such is the exact sense of the word used, Luke v. 29; xiv. 13), it must have been an evening meal. The discourse in reply to the objection and question of the Pharisees may have been spoken on the day following. It appears to have been interrupted by the urgent petition of Jairus. As the Lord was on His way to the ruler's house, the WOMAN WHO TOUCHED HIS GARMENT was healed. Before He reached the house the maiden was already dead. Jesus, having soothed the father's anguish and stayed his fainting faith with the command, "*Fear not, only believe,*" excluded from the chamber of death all witnesses, save the parents and His own most intimate friends. Then, with two simple words in the familiar mother tongue—"TALITHA CUMI!" ("Damsel, arise")—He forced death to relax its hold. As if this awe-inspiring miracle had been simply the most natural thing to do in the circumstances (as indeed to Him it was), He cut short all loud wonder and rapturous thanks by ordering food to be immediately administered, and enjoining silence. (Matt. ix. 18–26; Mark v. 22–43; Luke viii. 41–56.)

Our Saviour's careful discrimination of the conduct suited to each case should here be noted. The man who had been possessed with the legion was bidden to

94 *OUTLINES OF THE LIFE OF CHRIST.*

publish God's great mercy in a region as yet unvisited by Christ (Mark v. 20). The sufferer who (from perfectly innocent and praiseworthy motives) sought to steal a cure secretly, was made to confess it "before all the people," and received in public Christ's emphatic and gracious approval of her faith.[1] But the maiden of twelve years was tenderly shielded from the unwholesome glare of publicity, and her parents were bidden to treat as a sacred family secret the mighty work wrought in their home.

THE HEALING OF TWO BLIND MEN, and of A DUMB MAN possessed with a demon, the occasion of fresh blasphemies from the Pharisees, are here narrated by St. Matthew (ix. 27-34).

Jesus now determined to give one more opportunity for repentance and faith to those among whom the first thirty years of His life had been spent. NAZARETH is not expressly named, but it is evidently intended by "HIS OWN COUNTRY."[2] This visit is connected in St. Matthew's account (xiii. 53, 54) with the Day of Parables; in St. Mark's (v. 43; vi. 1) with the raising of Jairus's daughter: the two Gospels together thus indicate the order of events. We may well believe that over none of the lost sheep of the house of Israel did the heart of the Good Shepherd yearn more tenderly than over these old neighbours and acquaintances among whom His mother seems still to have been residing, as well as " His brethren and His sisters." He taught as He was wont in their synagogue on the Sabbath. Their obstinate unbelief —type of all those who so stumble at difficulties that they are blind to evidence—limited His exercise of miraculous power to the healing of a " few sick folk," and called forth His wonder; not the wonder of igno-

---

[1] The three Gospels all record this instance, and no other, of our Lord addressing any one by the term "daughter."

[2] We have no English equivalent for the Greek word, which might be freely rendered, "*His old home.*"

rance, excited only by novelty, but of deepest wisdom, which sees that man's power to resist God's truth and grace is none the less marvellous because unhappily so familiar. (Matt. xiii. 53–58; Mark vi. 1–6.)

Jesus now resumed His mission tours among "ALL THE CITIES AND VILLAGES, teaching in their synagogues and preaching the gospel of the kingdom, and healing every sickness and every disease among the people." The reason of this resumption of town and village work is naturally found in the advance of the season. The long summer drought was over, and the early rains had recalled the husbandman to his toil. Ploughing begins in Palestine after the "first rains" of September have softened the hard soil; sowing, after the fuller "second rains" of October. Both ploughing and sowing are continued far into the winter.[1] Between these "first" and "second" rains—speaking roughly, subject to the movable nature of the Jewish year and the variableness of seasons—fell the new year's day of the civil year (Feast of Trumpets), the great yearly fast of the Day of Atonement (Tisri 10th), and the most joyous of the great festivals, the Feast of Tabernacles. The same reason which caused Jesus to absent Himself from the following Passover (John vi. 4; vii. 1), would this autumn forbid His going up to the Feast of Tabernacles. Twelve months later, when the time drew near "that He should be received up, He stedfastly set His face to go to Jerusalem" (Luke ix. 51); and at the Feasts of Tabernacles, of Dedication, and of Passover, He accepted, with full foreknowledge of the issue, that conflict with the Jewish rulers which He avoided until His mission as Prophet and Teacher to the lost

---

[1] *Cyc. Bib. Lit.*, art. "Agriculture." Kitto's *Phys. Hist. of Pal.*, under the months of SEP. and OCT. These first and second autumnal rains are of course both included in the "early rain," as distinguished from the "latter," or spring rain.

96 OUTLINES OF THE LIFE OF CHRIST.

sheep of Israel was accomplished. His movements (we may be well assured) were governed not by any unworthy timidity, but by the necessities of His work. Inattention to the important difference between the SUMMER AND WINTER MINISTRY of our Lord, seems to have led to confused and inadequate views of His labours.

If, in accordance with their name Apostles, and the purpose of their ordination (Mark iii. 14), THE TWELVE were to receive some practical training for their future work ; as the proper scene of their mission would be not the beach, the open plain, or the mountain glens, but the towns and villages, so the proper season would be the winter months. Accordingly we find that the Master, after a remarkable exhortation to prayer (Matt. x. 36-38), having called His chosen twelve around Him, endowed them with " power and authority " to work miracles, and SENT THEM FORTH IN PAIRS (Mark vi. 7) " to preach the kingdom of God." St. Matthew (x. 5–42) records the solemn prophetic charge delivered on this occasion. This discourse (as Dr. Stier[1] has pointed out) is divided into three sections. The *first* refers to their trial mission, then commencing, which was strictly confined to Israel (verses 5-15); the *second*, to their future mission to all nations (verses 16-23); the *third*, to their position and that of Christians in after times as disciples of Christ, in a world which rejects Him (verses 24-42 ; compare Mark vi. 7-11; Luke ix. 1-5).

The Twelve set forth, and " went through the towns, preaching the Gospel, and healing everywhere " (Luke ix. 6; Mark vi. 12, 13). Meanwhile the Master continued His work of preaching and teaching

[1] See his forcible remarks on "that strange and wilful opinion which imputes to the Evangelist an elaboration into one discourse of many sayings uttered at many various times."— *Words of the Lord Jesus*, vol. ii. pp. 1-5.

in the cities (Matt. xi. 1); accompanied, we may conjecture, by some of those whom He afterwards sent out as preachers (Luke x. 1). No indication is given of the time when the Twelve were sent forth on their honourable and arduous mission. Their return took place shortly before a Passover (Mark vi. 30; John vi. 4). The passages just quoted, as well as the nature of the case, indicate a considerable interval of time between their departure and return. Perhaps we may conjecture that they set forth soon after the Feast of Tabernacles, when the people had returned to their homes.

This prolonged absence of the Apostles naturally coincides with and accounts for a blank in the Gospel narrative. To this interval we may conjecturally assign some OCCURRENCES and SAYINGS either PECULIAR TO ST. LUKE'S GOSPEL, or appearing as *duplicates* of similar passages in St. Matthew. These we may suppose to have been supplied by eye and ear witnesses other than Apostles.

Such are—the request of a disciple, not stated to be an apostle to be taught to pray, with Christ's answer (Luke xi. 1-13); the discourse concerning the prophet Jonah (xi. 29-36); the incident of Jesus dining at a Pharisee's table without washing, and the discourse thereon (xi. 37-54); the warning to the multitude against hypocrisy (xii. 1-12); Christ's refusal to act as a magistrate, with the discourse against covetousness (xii. 13-21). The discourse beginning Luke xii. 22 appears to have been addressed to the Apostles, since Peter's words are quoted in verse 41. But there is no objection to the supposition that here, as elsewhere, St. Luke is connecting various detached sayings by a thread of subject, not of outward circumstance (xii. 22-59).

We now come upon a group of connected events, including *the one miracle recorded by all the Evangelists:* viz., (1) the DEATH OF JOHN THE BAPTIST;

D

(2) the RETURN OF THE TWELVE; (3) the FEEDING OF THE FIVE THOUSAND; (4) the WALK ON THE WATER; and (5) the DISCOURSE AT CAPERNAUM, in consequence of which many of Christ's disciples forsook Him. The chronology of these events is indicated by St. John's brief statement (vi. 4)—"And THE PASSOVER, a feast of the Jews, was nigh." This agrees with St. Mark's reference to "the green grass" (Mark vi. 39; comp. John vi. 10).

The duration of John the Baptist's imprisonment is nowhere recorded. If the interpretations and calculations adopted in the foregoing pages are correct, it must have lasted the greater part of two years, from May A.D. 27, to the spring of A.D. 29, when he was put to death by the Tetrarch of Galilee, Herod Antipas. For, assuming that we have satisfactorily proved the Passover named in John vi. 4 to be that of A.D. 29 (and the *third* in our Lord's ministry), we infer the date of John's death from the following facts. The account of the imprisonment and murder of John is given in Matthew xiv. 1-11; Mark vi. 14-29; introduced in both cases with the statement that Herod, hearing the fame of Jesus, concluded that John was risen from the dead (comp. Luke ix. 7-9). Matthew relates that John's disciples, having buried his corpse, brought the tidings of his death to Jesus; and that after hearing of it, "Jesus departed thence by ship into a desert place apart" (xiv. 12, 13). Mark and Luke state this retreat to the desert to have been in company with the Twelve, immediately on their return from their mission (Mark vi. 30-32; Luke ix. 10). They had doubtless received instructions when first sent out, as to the time and place of their return. There is no improbability or difficulty in supposing that our Lord had a double object, and that while He saw that His Apostles, wearied with their work and excited with their success, needed rest and quiet, He had also in view the danger of a popular rising in consequence of the murder of John. The supposition that He was influenced by personal fear, we may silently dismiss; but nothing could have been more disastrous to His cause than that His name should have been made the rallying cry for a seditious outbreak. That this was no imaginary danger is proved by the fact, that the multitude who followed Jesus and His Apostles into their retirement, actually proposed to seize His person and proclaim Him king, whether He would or no (John vi. 15).

Here only, except in the history of our Lord's sufferings and resurrection, we find the fourth Gospel traversing ground already trodden by the first three. All four Evangelists narrate the miracle of feeding the multitude, and mention the number—" about five thousand." All mention the previous crossing of the lake. Luke fixes the scene of the miracle in the neighbourhood of "a city called Bethsaida." Luke's narrative stops short with the miracle. Matthew, Mark, and John all mention the retirement of Christ to the mountain for solitary prayer after He had sent away His disciples and dismissed the multitude. John alone records the intention of the people to proclaim Jesus king. All three relate the miracle of walking on the sea in the storm, but Matthew only mentions the rash faith and humiliating failure of Peter. (Matt. xiv. 13-34; Mark vi. 32-53; John vi. 1-12.)

This attempt of the excited Galilæans to compel Jesus to put Himself at their head as king was a repetition in a rough and humble fashion of the offer made to Him by the Tempter (Matt. iv. 8, 9; Luke iv. 5-8). In the preceding and following miracles we may recognize a no less striking correspondence and contrast with the two other temptations. He who in the wilderness had been vainly tempted to satisfy His own hunger by a miracle, is here seen in the wilderness satisfying by miracle the hunger of thousands. He who had been challenged to show Himself the Son of God by flinging Himself down through the air, is here seen walking on the waters, and controlling the raging winds and waves.

The narrative of the first two Gospels briefly summarizes the CONTINUANCE OF our Lord's MISSION WORK in the district known as the land of Gennesaret (Matt. xiv. 34-36; Mark vi. 54-56). St. John tells how some who had partaken the wondrous meal crossed the lake to the western shore next day, in quest of Jesus. They found Him, to their amazement, at Capernaum (John vi. 22-24). We may probably suppose the discourse in the synagogue at Capernaum (John vi. 59) to have been delivered on the following Sabbath, and may infer that our Lord and the Twelve came to Capernaum for the purpose of spending the Sabbath there. In this discourse (for the sake of which St. John appears to have recorded the foregoing miracles) Jesus asserted His claim on the absolute faith of His hearers, as sealed and sent by the Father to bestow resurrection and eternal life; and taught (though enigmatically) the mystery of His atoning death. He thus laid the axe to the root of those carnal expectations which had inspired the attempt to proclaim Him king; and consequently "many of His disciples," strangers to spiritual faith, took offence at this "hard saying," and renounced their discipleship (John vi. 25-66). This defection was the occasion of a remarkable CONFESSION OF FAITH by Peter, and a terrible warning from the lips of Christ (John vi. 67-71).

We may regard this Sabbath at Capernaum as marking THE CLOSE OF THE SECOND YEAR of our Lord's Ministry. It was a year of intense and marvellous activity. The open breach with the rulers at Jerusalem, which marked its commencement, rendered it useless for Jesus to revisit Jerusalem, but did not cripple His ministry in Galilee.

Among the most memorable and characteristic events of these twelve months were the ordination of the Twelve Apostles, and their subsequent mission; the message from John, and his death; "the day of parables;" and some of our Lord's greatest miracles, including two instances of raising the dead, the stilling of the storm, the walk on the water, and the feeding of the five thousand. The double shadow which fell on the close of this year of ministry, in the misguided attempt of the Galilæans to make Jesus king, and the defection of many of His disciples, indicated that the time was drawing near for the close of Christ's Galilæan ministry. For a season, however, it might still be said to those so long and abundantly favoured with His presence (as He said afterwards to the people of Jerusalem), "Yet a little while is the light with you. Walk while ye have the light" (John xii. 35).

SECTION III.

THIRD YEAR. A.D. 29-30.

(A.U.C. 782-3.)

"AFTER these things Jesus walked in Galilee: for He would not walk in Judæa because the Jews sought to kill Him" (John vii. 1). Probably for the first time since He was twelve years old, He abstained from attending the Passover in the Holy City. He appears to have continued His ministry in Galilee with unabated energy. The account in the first two Gospels of His ministry in the land of Gennesaret may cover some weeks of April and May (Matt. xiv. 35, 36; Mark vi. 54-56). As yet we find no token of diminished labour or declining popularity; or of any attempt on the part of the rulers to carry out in Galilee that murderous purpose which was cherished with growing malignity at Jerusalem. But the two signs indicated at the close of the last section —the tendency to insurrection, and the apostasy of professed disciples—could not be misread by Him "who knew what was in man." A marked change is soon perceptible in the narrative.

The closing year of our Lord's earthly life is divided into two halves by the Feast of Tabernacles, at which, after an interval (according to our reckoning) of eighteen months, He again visited Jerusalem. These two periods present some features of strong contrast. But one character common to both is, the extension of our Saviour's labours to the borders of heathendom. His own words define the limits of His personal ministry: He was "not sent but unto the lost sheep of the house of Israel" (Matt. xv. 24). But "other sheep" He had, not of that fold (John x. 16), over whom His heart yearned; and though the time was not yet for the glad tidings to be preached to all nations, we see Him stretching the bounds of His ministry as wide as was consistent with their maintenance. During this summer He visited the frontiers of Phœnicia and the neighbourhood of Cæsarea Philippi. During the winter and early spring, having closed His ministry in Galilee, He carried it on, apparently for a considerable period, in Peræa. During the whole of this year the Twelve were with their Master; and the indications of time and place are more numerous than in previous years.

We may dismiss from our minds as wholly imaginary the unkingly and distressing picture sometimes drawn of this period of our Saviour's life, depicting Him as a harassed and anxious fugitive, retreating from His persecutors as David from Saul, and seeking safety in obscurity. St. John's statement (vii. 1) shows that the Galilæan ministry continued for some considerable time after the feeding of the five thousand and the Sabbath at Capernaum. This perfectly accords with the first two Gospels (Matt. xiv. 34–36; Mark vi. 53–56). Certain occasions are mentioned when Jesus sought privacy, but with no indication that the motive was care for His own safety (Mark vii. 24; ix. 30). If He took a brief interval of rest, it was a preparation for renewed activity. When He finally quitted Galilee, it was to visit that very part of Herod's dominion in which John the Baptist had been imprisoned and slain; and by the preparatory mission of the seventy, He invested His ministry in Peræa with a kind of regal state. When urged by zealous disciples or officious strangers to take thought for His own safety, our Lord's replies showed how little room there was in His plans for any such considerations (Matt. xvi. 22, 23; Luke xiii. 31–33; John xi. 8–10). When the time came to meet not only danger, but the certainty of death, long foreseen and foretold, His calm determination filled His disciples with astonishment and dread (Mark x. 32). The truth is that personal safety lay for Jesus in publicity, not retirement. To the last, in Jerusalem the one difficulty which embarrassed the rulers in their murderous purpose was the fear of a popular rising on His behalf (Matt. xxvi. 5; Luke xxii. 2; John xi. 48; xii. 11, 19).

To prevent any such outburst (so disastrous to His true influence and work) while carrying on His ministry of teaching and healing, may have been far more difficult than we are apt to suppose; for the most ignorant could not but be impressed and excited by His miracles, while thoughtful minds must have seen in His doctrine the germs of a mighty social and religious revolution. The frightful incident of the MASSACRE OF THOSE GALILÆANS " whose blood Pilate had mingled with their sacrifices" (Luke xiii. 1), suggests that Jesus may have had other motives for refraining from visiting Jerusalem beside the hostility of the Jewish rulers. For it seems probable that it was at this Passover that this atrocious massacre took place. The mention of " sacrifices " proves it to have been at Jerusalem; and it is unlikely that Galilæans would have been at Jerusalem, or would have provoked the savage vengeance of the Roman governor, except at one of the great festivals.

To this summer we may assign the HEALING OF AN INFIRM WOMAN IN THE SYNAGOGUE, related by St. Luke without any note of time or place (xiii. 10–17). Likewise the remonstrance of the "Scribes and Pharisees who came from Jerusalem" against the disciples for violating the traditions of the elders by " EATING BREAD WITH UNWASHEN HANDS." Jesus not only defended His disciples (as He had done in reference to Sabbath observance), but exasperated the Pharisees by declaring that their human traditions made void the Divine law (Matt. xv. 1–20; Mark vii. 1–23).

The Galilæan ministry of Christ may be regarded as now virtually at an end, though He had not yet finally quitted Galilee. Leaving those familiar scenes in which His ministry—though so bitterly opposed by the Jewish rulers, so fruitlessly attended by ignorant and thoughtless crowds, so imperfectly understood even by His disciples—had nevertheless reaped no scanty harvest, while sowing the living seed of a richer harvest to be reaped by His Apostles, Jesus turned His steps northward. He first visited the frontiers of Phœnicia. Rest and privacy seem to have been the immediate object of this excursion, and He neither taught nor wrought miracles in public. But the importunate prayer of a heathen mother—"A WOMAN OF CANAAN," "a Syro-Phœnician by nation," on behalf of her afflicted daughter, won from Christ not only the blessing she implored, but a warm eulogy on her faith (Matt. xv. 21–28; Mark vii. 24–30). When we consider the spiritual significance of this miracle, and the value of the lessons treasured up for all ages in the story of it, we seem justified in supposing, that it was for the sake of this one work of mercy that our Saviour trod so far out of His ordinary path. We have no reason to suppose that He departed from the rule He had laid down for His Apostles, by entering into any city of the Gentiles. If (on the critical maxim that the more puzzling and improbable a reading is, the more likely it is to be true), we accept the reading adopted by modern editors (Mark vii. 31), "He went through Sidon to the Sea of Galilee," we must understand the territory, not the city. If so, our Lord now reached the northern limit of Palestine. We can only conjecture the object of so remarkable a journey to have been rest, privacy, and the relief of entire change of scene for the disciples as well as for Himself, not so much on account of past labours, exhausting though they had been, as in view of the tremendous strain of the approaching autumn, winter, and spring.

We next find our Saviour resuming His labours near the eastern or south-eastern shore of the Lake of Galilee, having journeyed "through the midst of the coasts[1] of DECAPOLIS" (Mark vii. 31). Of the numerous and varied miracles summarily indicated by Matthew xv. 30, Mark particularizes one,—THE HEALING OF A DEAF AND DUMB MAN, accompanied with an injunction to keep silence, which, however, he disobeyed (Matt. xv. 29-31; Mark vii. 31-37). In the same region apparently, and about the same time, Jesus finding Himself again surrounded by a hungry multitude, fed 4,000 WITH SEVEN LOAVES AND A FEW FISHES. This miracle is discriminated from the former one by Christ Himself, as though to fore-

---

[1] *I.e.* "Borders," including the sense of "district" or "region." The word "coast" is never used in A.V. for the sea-shore, except in Luke vi. 17. In Acts xxvii. 2, the Greek word simply means places or regions.

stall the attempts of modern critics to confound them (Mark viii. 19, 20). Having dismissed the multitude, He recrossed the lake with His disciples, to the neighbourhood of MAGDALA AND DALMANUTHA (Matt. xv. 32-39; Mark viii. 1-10).

After refusing the request, at once presumptuous and unbelieving, for A SIGN FROM HEAVEN, in which the Pharisees joined with their bitter foes the Sadducees, Jesus left these blind rulers of the blind to themselves, and recrossed to the eastern shore. On the voyage the Apostles showed themselves still but dull learners, by supposing that the Master's warning against THE LEAVEN OF THE PHARISEES was occasioned by their having forgotten to take bread. Slight as this incident is, it throws no faint light on both the need and the reality of the inspiration which qualified them for their labours from and after the Day of Pentecost. (Matt. xvi. 5-12; Mark viii. 14-21.)

AT BETHSAIDA, JESUS HEALED A BLIND MAN who was brought to Him. A village-suburb of the city Julias seems to be meant, as St. Mark says, "He took the blind man by the hand, and led him out of the village."[1] (Mark viii. 22-26.)

Continuing His journey northward, Jesus visited the neighbourhood of Philip's newly built city of CÆSAREA PHILIPPI. Here (St. Luke says, when He had been "alone praying,") He received a remarkable confession of faith, in which the ever-ardent Peter stood forward as spokesman for his brother Apostles, and was answered by Christ in those memorable words, remarkable not only as containing the first occurrence in the New Testament of the word "Ec-

[1] In A.V. "town;" so in verse 27. Our translators render this word (kōmè), sometimes "village," sometimes "town;" e.g., Matt. ix. 35; x. 11. They never use "town" for "city." In Mark i. 38, the Greek word literally means "village-city," q.d., unwalled town.

clesia," but on account of the sense put upon them by the Romish Church—"Thou art Peter, and upon this rock I will build My Church." This declaration must have profoundly impressed the minds of the disciples, since the word "Ecclesia" (or its Hebrew equivalent, if Christ was speaking Hebrew) was already a sacred term, as applied to the assembly of Israel. Vague but sublime visions of authority and dominion would present themselves to their imagination. The Master therefore followed this splendid prediction by a strict injunction to silence (Matt. xvi. 20; Mark viii. 30; Luke ix. 21).

"From that time forth began Jesus" to impart to the Twelve the terrible secret of His approaching rejection by the rulers at Jerusalem, His sufferings and death; foretelling, at the same time, His resurrection on the third day. Peter's remonstrance at what seemed so irreconcilable with the promise lately made to him, drew on him a severe rebuke. This took place in private; but shortly afterwards Jesus publicly warned His assembled hearers that the cost of discipleship was daily self-denial, even to the taking up of the cross. (Matt. xvi. 21-28; Mark viii. 31-38; ix. 1; Luke ix. 22-27.)

A week elapsed, and the Three who were admitted to closer fellowship with their Master than their brother Apostles were called to witness a spectacle, which seems to have impressed their minds more deeply than any other miracle, save the crowning miracle of the Resurrection. The Transfiguration of Christ is referred to by the Apostle Peter with solemn emphasis in his Second Epistle (i. 16-18). St. John, though the plan of his narrative allowed no place for relating this manifestation of Christ's glory, alludes to it in the introduction to his Gospel (i. 14). The mediæval tradition which assigned Mount Tabor as the scene of the Transfiguration, is now generally considered erroneous. Less than 1,900 feet high,

Tabor has no claim to be called "a high mountain," and is deficient in those circumstances of lonely grandeur suited to this sublime transaction, which are abundantly furnished by MOUNT HERMON.[1] The connection of the narrative agrees with the view that the holy mount was Hermon. The return from Philip's tetrarchy to Galilee seems indicated in Mark ix. 30 (Matt. xvii. 1-8; Mark ix. 2-8; Luke ix. 28-36).

Descending next day from the mountain, Jesus found the nine Apostles whom He had left below surrounded by an excited multitude, assailed with questions by the Scribes, and in perplexity and distress. In their Master's absence, they had tried to exercise the power, formerly given to them (Luke ix. 1), but had failed. The contrast between the calm, sublime communion with Heaven on the mount, and this scene of misery, confusion, and weakness, forced from our Saviour's lips a rare expression of the anguish and burden which He endured from the daily presence of sin and suffering. He revived the faith of the afflicted father, CAST OUT THE EVIL SPIRIT, and privately told His Apostles that their failure had been through lack of faith; at the same time warning them, that the faith needed for such works was itself no easy attainment, but to be sought "by prayer and fasting" (Matt. xvii. 14-21; Mark ix. 14-29; Luke ix. 37-43).

This narrative affords another indication that in this northern journey our Lord was not withdrawing from public labour. But on returning "through Galilee" to Capernaum, "He would not that any man should know it." Again He forewarned His disciples of His approaching sufferings, and foretold His resurrection. They were unable to believe that He really

[1] Dr. W. M. Thomson, however, thinks something may be said in favour of Mount Tabor (*The Land and the Book*, p. 433). For a description of Mount Hermon see *Tent Work*, vol. i., pp. 261, ff.

meant what His words seemed to mean, and (with natural inconsistency) "feared to ask Him." St. Matthew's phrase, "while they were sojourning in Galilee," seems to point to some continuance—possibly several weeks—of this quiet private life. (Matt. xvii. 22, 23; Mark ix. 30-32; Luke ix. 43-45.) This accords with the remonstrance of the unbelieving brethren of Jesus (John vii. 2-9) who urged Him to go up to the Feast of Tabernacles and "show Himself to the world." The Feast fell in that year in the middle of October. The narrative has therefore brought us again to the season when the "early rains" summoned the ploughman and the sower to their labour, and the time for great open-air gatherings was past. Jesus had no intention of continuing His ministry in Galilee into another winter. His work there was virtually ended.

To this period belongs the MIRACLE OF THE TRIBUTE MONEY (Matt. xvii. 24-27), and the discourse occasioned by the STRIFE FOR PRE-EMINENCE among the Twelve (Matt. xviii. 1-35; Mark ix. 33-50; Luke ix. 46-50).

Jesus went up to the FEAST "not openly, but as it were in secret," so as not even in appearance to ally Himself with the excitable, worldly-minded Galilæans, who would have "taken Him by force to make Him a king." Probably it needed the exercise of the greatest wisdom and self-restraint to guard against the danger of a popular uprising. The people were anxiously expecting Him at Jerusalem, but restrained from any open expression of opinion through fear of the rulers. Not until THE LAST DAY OF THE FEAST did Jesus appear in the Temple and resume His public teaching. His calm authority and courage struck the people with awe, and filled the rulers with alarm and rage. A year and a half had elapsed since His last visit; but His reference to the healing of the infirm man on the Sabbath shows how fresh the events of that time were in His hearers' memory as well as His own. Many believed on Him as the Christ, in the face of fierce opposition. The officers of the Sanhedrin sent to arrest Him felt the spell of His majestic presence and heart-searching words, and dared not execute their warrant. NICODEMUS raised an honest though feeble protest in His behalf, and the council broke up in confusion. (John vii. 10–53.)

Great critical difficulties, as is well known, beset the narrative of the WOMAN BROUGHT TO CHRIST FOR JUDGMENT (John viii. 2–11); greater, indeed, than affect any other passage in the New Testament. But these by no means constitute a reason for rejecting it as an authentic portion of the Gospel narrative, even if we suppose that it is inserted out of the chronological order,[1] or was added by another hand. It has been commonly taken for granted that St. John's narrative of this visit to Jerusalem extends to the close of chap. viii., if not further. But in chap. x. 22, we read, "*It was at Jerusalem, the Feast of the Dedication.*" A difficulty thus arises where to draw the line in the narrative between the two Feasts, and to which of them to assign the cure of the blind man. This difficulty vanishes if we suppose that the account of

[1] The difficulties attending this passage (including chap. vii. 53) arise not merely from the fact that it is wanting in a large number of MSS., including the oldest existing copies, while in some MSS. it is inserted at the end of the Gospel, or even at the close of Luke xxi.; but that the diction throughout is unlike St. John's, and that the variations in different copies are numerous and important. (See the statement of the whole question in Alford's Greek Testament.) Alford appears in error in appealing to the case of Stephen, in proof that the Romans by connivance permitted the Sanhedrin to inflict capital punishment. The Talmud states that "forty years before the destruction of the Temple, the power of inflicting capital punishment was taken away from Israel." Lightft. (*Horb. Heb.* vol. ii. p. 611) on John xviii. 31. "The stoning of Stephen was the illegal act of an enraged multitude." *Cyc. Bib. Lit.*, Art. "Sanhedrin." Cf. Conybeare and Howson, vol. i. p. 5.

the Feast of Tabernacles closes with chap. vii.; and that our Lord's words (viii. 12) contain an allusion to the Feast of Lights. On this view the whole of chaps. viii., ix., x. form one continuous section, belonging to the season of mid-winter.

At this point, therefore (viz., the close of John vii.), we return to the narrative of Matthew and Mark: for here Luke's Gospel parts company with theirs (ix. 51), rejoining them in the account of the final journey to Jerusalem (xviii. 15). Several important questions present themselves regarding the order of the history; to which the most discordant answers have been returned by harmonists and critics of equal eminence. Our only course therefore is carefully to examine and compare the Gospel narratives. Questions of this sort are not to be decided by authority, because where there is no *consensus*, but a conflict of authorities, it is really a more difficult task to apportion the relative weight of the authorities than to form a judgment on the original facts.

The first question is, did our Lord return to Galilee after the Feast of Tabernacles? Naturally He would do so, and we know of no reason why He should not. The first two Gospels state that Jesus " DEPARTED FROM GALILEE, and came into the coasts of Judæa beyond Jordan" (Matt. xix. 1; Mark x. 1). That is, He crossed the Jordan into Peræa, which was included in the tetrarchy of Herod Antipas, and was separated by the river from Galilee, Samaria, and Judæa. If He crossed into Peræa from Galilee, He must first have returned to Galilee from Jerusalem. Peræa was all but untrodden ground; and our Lord's purpose in visiting it was not to seek retirement, but to resume His public ministry. Crowds again gathered, and He both TAUGHT AND WROUGHT MIRACLES (Matt. xix. 2; Mark x. 1). St. John's statement (x. 40) that Jesus "went away AGAIN beyond Jordan," after the Feast of Dedication, implies that He was carrying on His ministry there previous to that feast, and thus confirms the account of the first two Evangelists.

St. Luke's Gospel contains four important statements peculiar to itself, bearing on this period of our Lord's ministry: (1) chap. ix. 51, 52; (2) chap. x. 1; comp. ver. 17; (3) chap. xiii. 22; (4) chap. xvii. 11. The first (somewhat too freely rendered in our A.V.) tells us that, "when the days were being fulfilled of His taking up" [*i.e.* into heaven], "He firmly fixed His face to journey to Jerusalem." The statement is not that the days were expired, but that they were in course of fulfilment; the appointed time had not arrived, but was drawing near. This statement may well be understood as covering the whole time from the Feast of Tabernacles to the Passover—the last half of the sacred year, the first half of the civil year. It seems best interpreted not of a single occasion, but of the high purpose and stedfast courage displayed in our Lord's *repeated visits* to Jerusalem during these months, accompanied by repeated warnings to His disciples that He was on His way to crucifixion. Great confusion and perplexity accrue when these words are supposed to form an introductory note of time to the whole following section of St. Luke's Gospel, as if chaps. x.–xviii. constituted a consecutive chronological whole. The difficulty vanishes if we take them as referring *generally* to the closing months of our Lord's ministry, but *immediately* to the incident which followed, ix. 52–56; and which is introduced in natural connection (not of time, but topic) with ver. 49, 50. On this view, no difficulty arises from the introduction in the chapters which follow of matter belonging to various dates. When the incident occurred, it is impossible to determine: possibly when our Lord was going up to the Feast of Dedication. We have no means of deciding whether the "messengers" were from among the Apostles or the Seventy, or other disciples.

The second passage (x. 1, ff.) relates to the appointment of SEVENTY PREACHERS, whom the Lord sent "two and two before His face into every city and and place, whither He Himself would come." This step, totally distinct in its bearings and motives from the appointment of the Twelve, was scarcely less important or significant. We gather from it, first, that our Lord's withdrawal from Galilee was of the nature not of a retreat, but of an advance. Feeling that His work there was accomplished, He would employ the brief remaining months of His earthly life in labours among towns and districts as yet unvisited. Secondly, that, having in view His final visit to Jerusalem, and the end which there awaited Him, Jesus deliberately invested the closing portion of His ministry with somewhat of the state and publicity of a royal progress, fitly closed in the appointed season by His triumphant entry into Jerusalem. Thirdly, that the number of towns and villages visited must have been very considerable, and, consequently, though the Seventy may have accomplished their work in two or three weeks, many weeks must have been occupied in the labours of which such solemn announcement was made. (Comp. xiii. 22.)

These inferences harmonize perfectly with the account in the first and second Gospels of the ministry in Peræa (Matt. xix. 1; Mark x. 1), which presents a strong contrast with the private journey to the Feast of Tabernacles (John vii. 10). Our previous conclusion is thus confirmed, that Jesus returned from Jerusalem to Galilee after that Feast, before making this new departure. It is conceivable that the Seventy may have been sent forth before the Feast; but it seems every way more probable that their mission was after the return of the people from the Feast. Reckoning the Feast to have closed on October 19th, and the Feast of Dedication to have fallen on December 19th, a clear month or six weeks might intervene between the return of the Seventy and the visit of Jesus to Jerusalem at the latter Feast (John x. 22). When our Lord returned after that Feast to Peræa (John x. 40), three months yet remained before the Passover, which was already approaching when He finally returned to Judæa, and for a brief season suspended His ministry and sought privacy and rest (John xi. 7, 54, 55).

When "THE SEVENTY RETURNED AGAIN with joy," their mission was accomplished. With this temporary character of their work correspond both the similarity and the contrast between the instructions given to them and the charge to the Twelve (comp. Luke x. 2-12, 16, with Matt. x. 5-42).

The third passage (Luke xiii. 22), which tells us how Jesus "went through the cities and villages, teaching and journeying towards Jerusalem," is sufficiently illustrated by the foregoing remarks. The special incidents with which it is connected (ver. 23, 31) may have occurred either before or after the Feast of Dedication.

The fourth passage (Luke xvii. 11; in which "THROUGH THE MIDST OF SAMARIA AND GALILEE" may be translated "BETWEEN SAMARIA AND GALILEE," *i.e.*, on the borders of the two districts) may possibly refer, not to our Lord's public ministry after the Feast of Tabernacles, but to His private journey to Jerusalem on occasion of that Feast (John vii. 9, 10).

Setting aside, then, as wholly untenable the notion that these passing references to time and place indicate the Evangelist's purpose to adhere to chronological order in the incidents and sayings collected in this part of his Gospel; and relinquishing as alike hopeless and useless the attempt to fit them, like bits of tesselated pavement, each into its exact place, we are warranted by the foregoing considerations in assigning to the closing six months of our

THIRD YEAR OF MINISTRY.

Lord's earthly life, the following matters recorded in the third Gospel:
The REFUSAL OF CERTAIN SAMARITAN VILLAGERS TO ENTERTAIN JESUS (chap. ix. 51–56); the REPROOFS addressed to two wavering disciples (vers. 59–62); the sending forth of the SEVENTY EVANGELISTS (x. 1–16), and THEIR RETURN (vers. 17–24); THE LAWYER'S QUESTION, answered by the parable of the GOOD SAMARITAN (vers. 25–37); the visit to the home of MARTHA AND MARY (vers. 38–42); Christ's reply to the question as to the FEWNESS OF [THE SAVED, and His answer (on the same day) when warned of HEROD'S THREATS, together with His LAMENT OVER JERUSALEM (xiii. 23–35); the HEALING on the Sabbath at the house of a Pharisee of a MAN WHO HAD DROPSY; and the parable of the GREAT SUPPER (xiv. 1–24); the warning concerning RASH DISCIPLESHIP given to the multitude (vers. 25–35); the three parables (in reply to the Pharisees' murmuring) of LOST AND FOUND (xv.); the parables of the UNJUST STEWARD, and of THE RICH MAN AND LAZARUS (xvi.); the parable of MASTER AND SERVANT, preceded by sayings concerning "offences" and "faith" (xvii. 1–10); the HEALING OF TEN LEPERS (vers. 11–19); the question and reply concerning THE KINGDOM OF GOD, followed by a brief discourse resembling part of Matt. xxiv. (vers. 20–37); and (lastly) the parables of the IMPORTUNATE WIDOW and the TWO WORSHIPPERS (xviii. 1–14). The labour which harmonists have bestowed in assigning to each of these sections its chronological place appears to be labour lost.

At this point LUKE'S narrative rejoins that of the earlier Gospels. The three Evangelists relate the incident—which has touched so deeply, and till the end of time will not cease to touch, the hearts of both parents and children—of THE CHILDREN BROUGHT TO JESUS; repulsed by His disciples, but invited, embraced, and blessed by the Master. Mark notices the displeasure of Jesus at this ungracious interference of the disciples. Their annoyance may be better understood if we suppose that the mothers brought their children into the house to which Christ and His Apostles had retired for food and rest, which seems indicated by the phrase with which Mark (x. 17) introduces the following incident,—"when He was gone forth into the way." (Matt. xix. 13–15; Mark x. 13–16; Luke xviii. 15–17.)

All three Evangelists likewise narrate the application of THE YOUNG RULER (who as a ruler of a synagogue could not have been a mere youth), and the conversation with the Apostles which followed. (Matt. xix. 16–30; Mark x. 17–31; Luke xviii. 18–30.) Matthew adds the parable of the LABOURERS IN THE VINEYARD (xx. 1–16). This portion of the synoptic narrative is doubtless to be assigned to the ministry in Peræa. But it seems impossible to decide whether its place is before or after the visit to Jerusalem in mid-winter recorded in the fourth Gospel. To that Gospel we now turn.

THE FEAST OF DEDICATION (John x. 22), or Feast of Lights, though not of Divine institution, yet possessed great national importance. It was instituted by Judas Maccabæus B.C. 164, in commemoration of the purification of the Temple after its desecration by Antiochus Epiphanes. It was celebrated eight days, commencing on the 25th of the 9th month (*Chisleu*). See 1 Mac. iv. 52–59; 2 Mac. x. 5–8. Fasting and mourning were forbidden. Palm-leaves and branches were borne by the worshippers in the Temple and synagogues. The houses in Jerusalem were illuminated as well as the Temple, whence the name "Feast of Lights."[1] This joyful national Festival, therefore, our Saviour recognized and honoured with His presence; and His reception

[1] *Cyc. Bib. Lit.*, Art. "Dedication" and "Festivals,' where authorities are fully given.

in Jerusalem was again such as compelled Him to seek more willing ears and obedient hearts elsewhere. It has been already suggested that the illumination of the Temple and city may have furnished the occasion of Christ's description of Himself as the LIGHT OF THE WORLD, and that consequently, chap. viii. 12—x. 40 of St. John's Gospel constitute a continuous narrative. This includes, first, a DISCOURSE, or rather discussion with the Phariseees, IN THE TEMPLE (viii. 12-20); followed by a second and more lengthened discussion also in the Temple, during which MANY BELIEVED ON HIM (ver. 30), but at the close of which His opponents tore up stones and WOULD HAVE STONED HIM to death; "but JESUS HID HIMSELF, and went out of the Temple, going through the midst of them, and so passed by." (John viii. 22-59.)

The HEALING OF ONE BORN BLIND (John ix.) was a glorious commentary on the claim of Jesus to be the "Light of the World," the spiritual significance of which is indicated by Christ Himself (ver. 5, 39–41). The rage of the Pharisees and rulers was intensified not only by the undeniable greatness of the miracle and the impression it produced, but by the fact that, like the cure of the impotent man (chap. v.), it was wrought on the Sabbath. St. John incidentally mentions that it had been already decreed by "the Jews"—*q.d.* the Sanhedrin—that any one who professed faith in Jesus as the Messiah should suffer excommunication. The closing verses (39–41) of ch. ix. belong more properly to the following chapter. The discourse of THE GOOD SHEPHERD (ch. x. 1-18) was probably spoken in the Temple, though this is not expressly stated. It produced a powerful impression even on some of the rulers (vers. 19-21; comp. vii. 50-52). The exact scene (the eastern colonnade or portico of the Temple-yard, or Court of the Gentiles, known as "Solomon's") as well as the season (ver. 22) is particularized by the Evangelist in recording the direct challenge given to Jesus by the Jewish authorities to say whether He was or was not THE CHRIST. Jesus in reply appealed to His former teaching and to His miracles, and declared His UNITY WITH THE FATHER. He was again threatened with stoning, and an attempt made to arrest Him; "but He escaped out of their hand." (Vers. 22-39.)

For a season our Lord resumed His ministry in PERÆA, at the very spot where John the Baptist had borne witness to Him. Crowds again gathered to hear Him, and "MANY BELIEVED ON HIM THERE." (Ver. 40-42.) The narrative thus brings us to the early weeks of A.D. 30. Three months yet remained before the Passover. It is therefore not improbable (as before pointed out) that to this period (January, February, or the early part of March) we should assign some of the events and sayings of the Peræan ministry recorded in the first three Gospels; specimens, few and brief, of those labours for which the mission of the Seventy had been the preparation. St. John's statement, concise as it is, shows that our Lord's withdrawal from Jerusalem involved no suspension or relaxation of His public labours.

From Peræa our Saviour was recalled to the neighbourhood of Jerusalem (against the remonstrances of His terrified disciples) by the illness and death of His beloved friend LAZARUS. After the great miracle of THE RAISING OF LAZARUS, He did not recross Jordan, but withdrew with His disciples "into a city called EPHRAIM," bordering on the wilderness of Judæa; identified by geographers with *Ophrah of Benjamin*, situate on a lofty hill-summit, five or six miles N.E. of Bethel; and represented by the modern village of Taiyebeh.

The PASSOVER was now so near at hand, that, according to custom (comp. Jos. *Ant.* xvii. 9 : 3; *Wars*, ii. 1 : 3), multitudes were already resorting to

Jerusalem in preparation for the Feast. Meantime the Sanhedrin, led by the counsel of the High Priest CAIAPHAS, were maturing their plans for the destruction of Jesus. He, attended by His chosen Twelve in the quiet retirement of Ephraim, allowed Himself a short breathing space, in preparation for the conflict which He knew awaited Him. This WITHDRAWAL TO EPHRAIM, therefore, marks the CLOSE OF OUR SAVIOUR'S PUBLIC MINISTRY, save those last days during which it behoved Him at JURUSALEM to show Himself publicly as Messiah, to deliver His final prophetic warnings in the Temple and farewell words to His disciples, and to fulfil the unconscious prophecy of Caiaphas by dying, "not for that nation only, but that also He should gather together in one the children of God that were scattered abroad." (John xi. 47-57.)

From Ephraim, then, our Lord made that FINAL JOURNEY TO JERUSALEM by way of JERICHO, which is recorded by the first three Evangelists. St. Mark, in his graphic way, depicts the calm courage of the Master and the terror and perplexity of His followers: "Jesus went before them: and they were amazed; and as they followed, they were afraid" (x. 32). On this journey, Christ again foretold to His disciples in the plainest terms His approaching sufferings and resurrection; but "they understood none of these things." It remained to them such an incomprehensible mystery, on the one hand, that Jesus should go to Jerusalem at all, if He foresaw that He would be seized and crucified; or, on the other hand, that He who had quelled the storm, controlled demons, conquered death itself, could possibly fall a victim to so horrible a fate, that they persuaded themselves His words must conceal some other meaning than that ghastly and incredible one they literally expressed. (Matt. xx. 17-19; Mark x. 32-34; Luke xviii. 31-34.)

THE AMBITIOUS REQUEST OF ZEBEDEE'S SONS, and of their mother on their behalf, is more easily intelligible, if we take John xix. 25 (as compared with Matt. xxvii. 56, and Mark xv. 40) to imply that Salome, wife of Zebedee, was sister to our Lord's mother. As first cousins, and as having always been, with Peter, the special chosen companions of Jesus, they might suppose they had a claim to which even Peter's must yield. (Matt. xx. 20-28; Mark x. 35-45.)

All three Gospels relate the visit of Jesus to JERICHO, and THE HEALING OF A BLIND MAN, whom Mark calls Bartimæus. Matthew says there were two blind men, which occasions no difficulty; but there is a perplexing though slight discrepancy in Luke's account. Mark expressly describes the miracle as having been wrought as our Lord, with His disciples and a great crowd, *came out* of Jericho. Luke says the blind man was sitting by the wayside as Jesus *drew near* to Jericho, and gives the impression that the cure was wrought before He entered the city. The ancient and obvious solution is, that the "two" mentioned by Matthew were healed, one as Jesus entered the town, the other as He left it. The difficulty in the way of this explanation is the close identity of the words used in each case, and the unlikelihood that in both cases the multitude should have rebuked the blind man for his loud cries for help. Yet it must be confessed that there is nothing but what might have naturally happened in any case; and it would not have been surprising had there been half a dozen blind beggars at each gate, at a time when such multitudes were going up to Jerusalem. It does not seem possible to maintain the explanation (favoured by Dr. Robinson) that instead of "*As He was come nigh,*" we may translate, "*As He was still nigh*"—*i.e.* after quitting Jericho. Some simple circumstance which the wonted brevity of the Gospel narrative suppresses, might perhaps clear up the whole difficulty: as, *e.g.*, if the first beggar *followed Jesus* through Jericho, and was healed, *with the second*, as He came out; or if the application of the second was occasioned by his hearing of the cure of the first. (Matt. xx. 29–34; Mark x. 46–52; Luke xviii. 35—xix. 1.)

St. Luke alone relates the story of ZACCHÆUS, "chief among the publicans" (*i.e.* chief collector of taxes), at whose house our Saviour, to the amazement and indignation of many probably beside the Pharisees, took up His abode for the night (Luke xix. 2–10). On this occasion He spoke the parable of THE POUNDS, closely resembling that of the Talents, delivered the following week at Jerusalem. While these tremendous words, foreshadowing the kingly "wrath" prophesied of in Ps. ii., were yet ringing in the ears of the trembling disciples, "He went before, ascending up to Jerusalem." (Ver. 11–28.) To His eye, though to no other, the end to which He was moving was full in view as they climbed that steep and desolate pass,—the "baptism" of suffering of which a few days before He had spoken. (Matt. xx. 22. Compare Luke xii. 50.)

At this solemn crisis in the history all four Gospels converge. THE TRIUMPHAL ENTRY INTO THE HOLY CITY which they all narrate, with the subsequent exercise of "authority" in the Temple, angrily but vainly challenged by the rulers (Matt. xxi. 23), constituted a public unmistakable assertion of the claim of Jesus to be what the multitude proclaimed Him— "the Son of David," "the King of Israel coming in the name of the Lord." Every circumstance of this entry was deliberately arranged so as to indicate its importance and significance. The disciples who were sent, not to ask as a favour, but to claim as a royal right, the use of the colt "whereon never man sat," were directed to say, "The Lord hath need of him."

122 OUTLINES OF THE LIFE OF CHRIST.

Notice of the intention of Jesus was conveyed to the city, so that "much people" went forth to meet Him, bearing palms, as at the Feast of Dedication and on other joyful occasions. When appealed to by some of the Pharisees to rebuke the enthusiasm of His disciples, who mingled their hosannas of welcome with a solemn chant of praise to God, Christ in the most emphatic manner sanctioned their conduct. The deliberate fulfilment of prophecy (Zech. ix. 9) noticed both by Matthew and John, must lose both meaning and majesty to the English reader if he fails to bear in mind that in the sentiment, history, and sacred literature of Israel, the horse was regarded as a war-like beast (whose use was therefore discountenanced by the law, Deut. xvii. 16), and that the ass, instead of being, as with us, the despised drudge of the poor, was treated with high regard, as suited to the peaceful use of chieftains and judges. (Comp. Gen. xxii. 3; Judges v. 10; x. 3, 4; xii. 14; 2 Sam. xvii. 23.) The purpose alike of the prophecy and of its voluntary fulfilment, was to present the promised King of Israel as no warlike despot, but a peaceful and just ruler. (Comp. Heb. vii. 2; Ps. lxxii. 2, 4, 7.)

St. John fixes the time of our Lord's arrival at Bethany: "six days before the Passover" (xii. 1). The Passover being the 14th Nisan (Lev. xxiii. 5), the sixth day before it was Nisan 8. If, therefore, the Passover was on Thursday (the proof of which we shall presently consider), our Lord reached Bethany on Friday, probably at least three hours before sunset (Jos., *Ant.* xvi. 6:2), so as to spend the Sabbath with His friends. This Sabbath was Nisan 9th; Saturday, April 1st, of our calendar. St. John's phrase "They made Him a supper," indicates something beyond the common evening meal: an entertainment in His honour, to which other guests as well as His disciples were bidden. This would naturally fall in with the custom of making the evening meal after the Sabbath a fuller and more generous meal than ordinary. Consequently the statement (John xii. 12) that the triumphal entry into Jerusalem took place "*the next day*," must mean the next day, not after the arrival at Bethany, but after the Sabbath. It has, however, been inferred by many critics from Matt. xxvi. 2-6; Mark xiv. 1-3, that the supper at Bethany was only two days before the Passover. This view, which makes the fourth Gospel contradict the other two, is totally unnecessary, inasmuch as in both Matthew and Mark the general statement that the Feast took place *while Jesus was in Bethany*, is unconnected with the reference to the two days, and may with perfect propriety be retrospective, referring to what had taken place three days earlier.

St. Luke, having recorded the earlier anointing by that unnamed penitent whom tradition has confounded with Mary Magdalene (omitted in the other Gospels), abstains from any reference to the anointing at Bethany, and consequently to the supper. The other three Gospels as naturally omit the earlier occurrence. John alone gives the name of her to whom Christ promised immortal remembrance; just as he alone gives the name of the high-priest's servant whose ear was cut off, and tells who it was that struck the blow. The reason in each case may have been, that the persons named were no longer living.

On the first day of the week, therefore, Sunday, Nisan 10th, our Lord made His entry into Jerusalem. He saw reason to defer it until afternoon, so that by the time He reached the Temple, sunset was already approaching (Mark xi. 11: comp. i. 32), and the market, which He found in full activity the following morning, was over, or nearly so, for the day. He therefore merely "looked round about upon all things," and returned with the Twelve to Bethany. The incidents mentioned by St. Matthew, to wit, the miracles wrought in the Temple on THE BLIND AND THE LAME, and THE HOSANNAS OF THE CHILDREN, which offended the priests, may perhaps belong to this (*Sunday*) afternoon.

On the morrow, Monday, Nisan 11th, Jesus returned to the City, and entered the Temple about sunrise. The market which profaned the great outer court, by suppressing which Jesus had signalized His entrance on the prophetic office, three years before, was again in full activity; and the near approach of the festival would naturally cause the number both of sellers and buyers to be specially numerous. The same motives which prompted the first, prompted even more urgently the SECOND CLEANSING OF THE TEMPLE (Matt. xxi. 12, 13; Mark xi. 15–19; Luke xix. 45–48). The three Evangelists who narrate this are silent concerning the first cleansing, which lay entirely out of the scope of their narrative. On the other hand, St. John, whose plan required him to record the first cleansing, had no occasion to mention the second. This solemn vindication of the honour of even that portion of His Father's house which was open as a place of prayer to "all nations," was appropriate alike to the commencement and to the close of our Saviour's ministry. Its repetition gave a double edge to the rebuke thus inflicted on the spiritual deadness which underlay the elaborate ritualism and hair-splitting scruples of the Rabbins.

An apparent discrepancy between the accounts of Matthew and Mark requires notice. Matthew's account, taken alone, would convey the impression that our Lord cleansed the Temple on the same day on which He entered Jerusalem (xxi. 12); and that it was on the following morning (ver. 18) that He pronounced the CURSE ON THE BARREN FIG-TREE. Mark, on the other hand, explicitly states, that as it was evening (xi. 11) when Jesus reached the Temple, He merely "looked round upon all things," and returned to Bethany; that the fig-tree was cursed the next morning; and that on that day (*Monday*) the Temple was cleansed. On the third morning (*Tuesday*) the fig-tree was seen withered. (Ver. 12, 15, 19, 20.) The explanation of this seeming discrepancy is simple. Mark's phrase (ver. 12), "*on the morrow,*" is a definite and careful note of time. Matthew's phrase, "*in the morning*" (xxi. 18), is indefinite, simply meaning, "early," "towards sunrise." Matthew records, in his condensed way, the facts, without regard to the several days; but he in no wise contradicts the orderly and explicit narrative of Mark. (Matt. xxi. 12–22; Mark xi. 12–26.)

On the third day of the week JESUS WAS QUESTIONED by the representatives of the Sanhedrin as to His authority; and in reply asked them a question concerning the authority of John the Baptist which they declined to answer. (Matt. xxi. 23–27; Mark xi. 27–33; Luke xx. 1–8.) With this incident Matthew connects the parable of the TWO SONS (ver. 28–32); that of the WICKED HUSBANDMEN, related also by Mark and Luke; that of the MARRIAGE FEAST and WEDDING GARMENT, given by him only. Matt. xxi. 33—xxii. 14; Mark xii. 1–12; Luke xx. 9–19.) Let the reader not fail to mark the repeated indications that, up to this period, the regard in which Jesus was held by the people, was so great as to form the one dangerous hindrance to the plots of the authorities against Him. See Matt. xxi. 46; xxvi. 5; Mark xi. 18; xii. 12; xiv. 2; Luke xix. 47, 48; xx. 26; xxii. 2; John xii. 19. The fear of rescue may have been the leading motive which prompted them (contrary to their own prudent resolution), when Jesus was in their hands, to hurry forward with profane indecency His condemnation and execution on the feast day. Our Lord's own words, John x. 18, were literally true, even apart from any exercise of miraculous power. It needed but a word from Him to have filled Jerusalem with insurrection and bloodshed.

126 OUTLINES OF THE LIFE OF CHRIST.

The following events and sayings belong to these closing days of Christ's public ministry. (1) The attempt first of the Pharisees and then of the Sadducees to entangle Jesus by questions concerning THE PAYMENT OF TRIBUTE, and the RESURRECTION. (Matt. xxii. 15–33; Mark xii. 13–27; Luke xx. 20–40.) (2) THE SCRIBE'S QUESTION and Christ's memorable answer, defining the foundation of Christian ethics. (Matt. xxii. 34–40; Mark xii. 28–34.) Compare the somewhat similar incident (Luke x. 25–28). (3) Christ's question concerning Messiah being the SON AND YET LORD OF DAVID. (Matt. xxii. 41–46; Mark xii. 35–37; Luke xx. 41–44.) (4) THE DISCOURSE AGAINST THE SCRIBES AND PHARISEES, addressed to the "multitude and to His disciples," of which Mark and Luke give only a brief epitome. (Matt. xxiii.; Mark xii. 38–40; Luke xx. 45–47.) Matthew's report of this tremendous discourse winds up with a lament over Jerusalem, resembling that which Luke records as uttered at an earlier period (xiii. 34, 35). The approval of the WIDOW'S OFFERING. (Mark xii. 41–44; Luke xxi. 1–4.) Mark incidentally notices that Jesus was SITTING " over against the treasury ; " *q.d.*, in that part of the court known as the women's court, in which the collecting boxes stood to receive offerings. The Rabbins tell us that none might *sit* in the Temple but a Prince of the House of David.

To these incidents St. John adds the request of CERTAIN GREEKS to see Jesus; the witness rendered to Jesus (for the third time) by A VOICE FROM HEAVEN; the CLOSING WORDS OF CHRIST; and HIS DEPARTURE FROM THE TEMPLE (xii. 20–36). The Temple, indeed, is not expressly named here by St. John, but we can scarcely err in understanding it to be referred to. The Evangelist adds a kind of summary of the whole history up to this point; and the words of Christ which he quotes (ver. 44–50) may have been uttered at any time, though probably on one of these closing days.

"Jesus went out, and departed from the Temple" (Matt. xxiv. 1; Mark xiii. 1). He left behind Him the Past, with its gorgeous ritual intact, but with the doom of death invisibly written upon Temple, Priesthood, and Commonwealth. He carried with Him the light and life, the promise and living seed, of the Future. He appears to have left the Temple by the eastern gate, and crossed the bridge which spanned the valley of Kedron; for immediately afterwards we find Him seated with His disciples on the Mount of Olives in full view of the Temple (Matt. xxiv. 3; Mark xiii. 3). No touch of decay had as yet stained its unrivalled magnificence. As the sun went down behind it, causing the glorious pile to stand out a dark mass against the sky, One only knew that the sound of His departing footsteps had been the knell of its glory; One only, looking across the gulf of forty years, could behold it vanishing in blood and fire. Questioned by His disciples as to the meaning of the terrible words spoken as He quitted it (Matt. xxiv. 2; Mark xiii. 2; Luke xxi. 5, 6), Jesus delivered His PROPHECY OF THE DESTRUCTION OF JERUSALEM and of "the end of the world" (Matt. xxiv. 4–41; Mark xiii. 4–33; Luke xxi. 9–33). This was followed by warnings to maintain watchfulness, enforced by a brief parable given by Mark only (xiii. 34), and by the parables of the TEN VIRGINS and the TALENTS, and the description of the FINAL JUDGMENT commonly though inaccurately referred to as "the parable of the Sheep and Goats." (Matt. xxiv. 42—xxv. 46; Mark xiii. 33–37; Luke xxi. 34–36.)

It has been commonly assumed that our Lord finished His public ministry on the third day of the week, and that the Wednesday, of which on that supposition we have no account, was spent in retirement at Bethany. This, however, is open to question. St. Luke's statement (chap. xxi. 37, 38) naturally suggests a longer period than two days. It is difficult to believe that our Lord would have closed His ministry a day earlier than necessary. St. Matthew tells us that "When Jesus had finished all these sayings, He said unto His disciples, Ye know that after two days is the Passover." St. Mark gives a corresponding statement (Matt. xxvi. 1, 2; Mark xiv. 1). In both passages our translators have interposed the words "*the feast of*," which if they were in the Greek text would decide what at present seems doubtful. For although the Passover lamb was slain on Nisan 14th the festival did not begin till sunset, when the 15th Nisan began. The Passover supper was eaten *in the night* following the 14th, namely, after sunset (Ex. xii. 6–8). Although, therefore, our Lord does not expressly use the word "feast," yet the most natural interpretation of His words is, that He is speaking not of the 14th, on which the leaven was put away and the paschal lamb sacrificed, but of the 15th Nisan, the first day of the festival. Assuming (see Part IV., sec. 1) that He kept the true Passover with His disciples, and that the Friday on which He was crucified was Nisan 15th, it is evident that the words "after two days" (*i.e.*, "the day after tomorrow") must have been spoken not on Tuesday, the 12th, but on Wednesday, the 13th, which is therefore indicated as THE CLOSING DAY of our Saviour's ministry.

That the day was reckoned from sunset in the time of Moses, is evident from Ex. xii. 18, 19, though a question has been raised on this point. (See *Cyc. Bib. Lit.*, Art. "Day.") The lamb was to be slain "between the two evenings" (Ex. xii. 6; Levit. xxiii. 5). The meaning of this phrase appears to be "at sunset"—the *first evening* being when the sun begins to set, the *second* the twilight after sunset. So Deut. xvi. 6, "*at even, at the going down of the sun*" (compare ver. 4). In Lev. xxiii. 5, the Passover is stated to be "*in the 14th of the first month, between the two evenings*" (where our A.V. has omitted to give the literal rendering in the margin); but this must be interpreted in accordance with ver. 32, which, in like manner, describes the Day of Atonement (10*th* *Tisri*) as "*in the 9th of the month, at even, from even to even.*" (See Wieseler, p. 315 ; McClellan, p. 475, 476.) The Karaites and other later Jewish authorities (quoted by Rosenmüller on Ex. xii. 6) seem therefore to have been more correct in their interpretation of the original law than the Pharisees. But, in point of fact, in our Saviour's time the paschal lambs were killed and sacrificed in the Temple "between the ninth and eleventh hours" (3 to 5 p.m.). (Jos. *Wars*, vi. 9 : 3.) The Mishna states that the daily evening sacrifice was slain half an hour after the 8th hour, *i.e.*, at Paschal tide about 2.30 p.m., and sacrificed half an hour after the 9th hour, *i.e.*, about 3.30 p.m.; but on the day before the Passover (*i.e.*, on Nisan 14th) it was slain and sacrificed an hour earlier, to give time for slaying and sacrificing the paschal lambs. The worshipper slew the lamb, and a priest received the blood in a bowl, and handed it on to the priest whose office it was to pour it out before the altar. This, with the burning of the appointed parts on the altar, constituted the SACRIFICE (Pesachim, ch. v. 6, 10). The SUPPER, which was the feast on the sacrifice, was the beginning of the "Feast" or "Festival" of unleavened bread (Ex. xiii. 6, 7 ; Lev. xxiii. 5-8 ; 2 Chron. xxx. 13-22), to the whole seven days of which the name "Passover" is given in modern Jewish almanacks.

PART IV.
CONCLUSION OF THE GOSPEL HISTORY.

SECTION I.

THE SUFFERINGS OF CHRIST.

NISAN 14 AND 15; APRIL 6 AND 7, A.D. 30 (A.U.C. 783).

TWO days after Jesus closed His public ministry occurred THE PASSOVER and the days of unleavened bread. So the first two Gospels tell us (Matt. xxvi. 1, 2; Mark xiv. 1). The third Gospel simply says, "The festival drew near of the Passover and of the days of unleavened bread" (xxii. 1). The Sanhedrin, assembled in the palace of the high-priest Caiaphas, agreed that the risk of a popular outbreak was too great to admit of their arresting Jesus during the festival; but their plans were destined to be overruled through the treachery of Judas and the force of circumstances. (Matt. xxvi. 3–5, 14–16; Mark xiv. 1, 2, 10, 11; Luke xxii. 2, 6.)

"The day of unleavened bread, on which the Passover must be sacrificed," arrived (Luke xxii. 7). "On the first day of unleavened bread, when they were wont to sacrifice" (or "were sacrificing") "the Passover, His disciples say to Him, Where wilt Thou that we go and make ready that Thou mayest eat the Passover?" (Mark xiv. 12; Matt. xxvi. 17.) In reply to this question Jesus commanded two of His disciples, Peter and John, to go into the city, and to say to the master of the house to which He directed them, "The Master saith, My time is at hand; I will keep the Passover at thy house, with My disciples." "Where is the guest-chamber where I shall eat the Passover with My disciples?" "And the disciples did as Jesus had appointed them; AND THEY MADE READY THE PASSOVER." (Matt. xxvi. 17–19; Mark xiv. 12–16; Luke xxii. 8–13. N.B.—The last words are common to the three Gospels.) "And WHEN THE HOUR WAS COME, He sat down" (lit., "lay down," or "reclined"), "and the twelve Apostles with Him. And He said unto them, With desire I have desired to eat THIS PASSOVER with you before I suffer." (Luke xxii. 14, 15; comp. Matt. xxvi. 20; Mark xiv. 17.) All the circumstances described in the Gospels correspond with the traditional accounts of the paschal supper.

It is undeniable that, had it been the intention of the three Evangelists to state in a manner that should preclude all doubt or controversy, that our Saviour kept the legal passover at the appointed time, they could not (in so brief compass) have used more plain, exact, or positive language. To suppose that the real fact which they meant to relate was, that Jesus, having by some means procured a lamb on the evening of the day preceding that on which the paschal lamb was killed, celebrated a sort of imitation paschal meal (which neither His disciples nor any one else would regard as a real and lawful Passover), is to suppose either that they were all three guilty of obscurity beyond example, if not of wilful misrepresentation, or else that they were mistaken. But this is a matter in which it was simply impossible, even after a lapse of years, for eye-witnesses to be mistaken. To suppose the three Evangelists mistaken, therefore, necessarily implies that the first Gospel was not written by an Apostle, and that the writers of the second and third did not derive their accounts from eye-witnesses.

Yet this is the alternative which a formidable array of Biblical critics and commentators, many of them as distinguished for piety as for scholarship, have striven to force on the belief of the Christian Church, on the ground of a supposed irreconcilable discrepancy between the three " synoptic " Gospels and the fourth Gospel. St. John's Gospel, it is maintained, shows that the day of the Crucifixion was the 14th Nisan, the day on which the paschal lambs were sacrificed; and that the Last Supper therefore took place on the evening of Nisan 13th. It has even been suggested that St. John wrote his account to correct the error into which his predecessors had fallen.

We have therefore now to examine the account in the fourth Gospel. (1) St. John tells us (xiii. 1), "Before the festival of the Passover, Jesus, knowing that His hour was come that He should depart out of the world unto the Father, having loved His own who were in the world, He loved them unto the end." Two things are here affirmed: 1st, that Jesus knew before the Passover festival that the time of His departure was come; 2nd, that this foresight did not hinder the warm, full flow of His love to His own; it glowed unquenched to the last. (Comp. chap. xv. 9-13.) There is nothing here to imply that the supper which St. John goes on to describe was other than the paschal meal. On the contrary, the opening of the next verse, "And supper being come,"[1] naturally looks back to the word "Passover," and implies that the paschal supper is meant. In a sense, however, the Passover *supper* might be said to be before the

[1] Not "*being ended.*" The reading of modern editors is, "*during supper.*" The received reading has the same force as in Mark xiv. 17, "evening having come."

festival. The English reader must bear in mind that the word "feast" means not *a meal,* but a *festive season,* including in this case a whole week. The law of Moses, though reckoning the day to begin at sunset, yet connects (apparently in popular language) the night with the day preceding. The 15th Nisan, therefore, and with it the festival of the Passover, or of unleavened bread, might be popularly regarded as beginning at sunrise rather than sunset.

(2) St. John tells us that those who brought Jesus from Caiaphas to Pilate "went not into the judgment hall" (or Governor's palace), "lest they should be defiled, but that they might eat the Passover." Hence it is argued that the time of eating the Passover had not yet arrived. But the defilement contracted by entering a heathen's house would not have lasted beyond sunset. (Levit. xxii. 6–9; Lightfoot, *Hor. Heb.;* and Wieseler, p. 351.) There would therefore have been no hindrance to their eating the paschal meal, if it was not due till the following evening. On the same day, in the afternoon, Joseph of Arimathea "went in boldly to Pilate." (Mark xv. 43.) But (as was long ago pointed out by Lightfoot) the term "Passover" included not only the lamb, but the peace-offering called "*chagigah,*" *i.e.* "festivity" or "festive offering." To this the Rabbins apply the reference in Deut. xvi. 2, to "the herd" as well as "the flock." The Mishna (Pesachim, chap. vi. p. 112; De Sola's Trans.) gives rules as to when the festive offering might be sacrificed on the 14th, and eaten with the paschal supper. But the regular time was the morning of the 15th. Legal defilement therefore would have debarred from this important part of the Passover festivity. Another explanation, given by Chrysostom (McClellan, p. 487), and maintained with much force and clearness by Dr. Milligan (*Contemporary Review,* August, 1868), is that the priests had actually not eaten the paschal supper, owing to

their having spent the night in planning and carrying out the arrest of Jesus, and in the proceedings which followed. But they could not eat it before sunrise, now near at hand; and if they meant to eat it in the evening, the remarks already made as to defilement would apply. The former explanation therefore appears decidedly preferable.

(3) Pilate's offer to release Jesus, according to the custom that he should release a prisoner "in the Passover" (John xviii. 39), implies that the Passover feast had begun. This seems decisive as to St. John's view of the day.

(4) "*It was the preparation of the Passover.*" (Ch. xix. 14.) It is urged that this phrase can mean nothing but "*the eve of the Passover*"—that is, Nisan 14th—and that therefore, according to St. John, the Crucifixion took place on that day. But (*a*) this statement is unsustained by any evidence beyond the dogmatic (sometimes vehement) assertion of certain eminent scholars. "Not one single example can be brought to prove this usage." (Wieseler, p. 310.) (*b*) If the phrase had this meaning, it could be only in reference to the *afternoon* of the 14th; but St. John is here speaking of the morning. (*c*) " Preparation " (Paraskeuè) was the regular name for the 5th day of the week—Friday. This is proved with abundant learning by Dr. Milligan. St. Mark thus explains the word (ch. xv. 42; comp. Matt. xxvii. 62; Luke xxiii. 54); and so St. John himself uses it in ver. 31, 42.

(5) A difficulty has been found in the statement (ver. 31) respecting the day following the Crucifixion —" *That Sabbath day was a high day.*" But it might well be so regarded ; for it was the day (16th Nisan) on which the sheaf of first-fruits, cut with great solemnity after sunset of the 15th, was offered with rejoicing in the Temple.

(6) Another objection has been raised with reference

THE SUFFERINGS OF CHRIST. 135

to the statement (ch. xiii. 29) that when Judas left the guest-chamber, some of the apostles supposed that he was gone to buy provisions for the feast. This, it is urged, he could not have done on the 15th Nisan. But the Divine law (Ex. xii. 16) makes an express distinction in regard to the preparation of food between the feast-day and the weekly Sabbath. The oral law recognizes this distinction. The Mishna ingeniously provides, that though food may not be bought on the feast day, a butcher *may divide his meat among his customers; and a person may go to a shop at which he is accustomed to deal and ask for what he requires.* (Yom. Tob, ch. iii.) But, in fact, in reading the minute subtleties and solemn trifling of the Mishnaic doctors, and their incessant disputes, it is difficult to imagine that much attention was paid to these regulations except by rigid Pharisees. This, indeed, is implied in John vii. 49.

The testimony of the fourth Gospel is thus found (notwithstanding the vehement stress laid by many distinguished scholars on the objections we have examined) to agree with that of the other three in fixing FRIDAY, Nisan 15th, as the day of the Crucifixion. The so-called discrepancies admit of solutions so easy and satisfactory that it is little less than marvellous that on so narrow a foundation so vast a superstructure of learned criticism has been raised.

A difficulty which deserves serious consideration, bearing not upon one Gospel only, but upon all, presents itself in the fact that, according to the traditions preserved in the Talmud, it was contrary to Jewish law to try a capital cause during the night, to pass capital sentence on the same day on which the criminal was tried, or to hold a court on a feast day. (See Lightfoot, *Hor. Heb.* on Matt. xxvii., and on John xix.; Wieseler, pp. 331–334.) But it would show great ignorance of human nature and history to suppose that the priests and their coadjutors, when they had in their power the hated Nazarene, whose death had long ago been decreed, would be withheld from their purpose by punctilios of legal etiquette, especially in days when the high-priesthood itself passed from hand to hand, in utter contempt of all legality, as the prize of ambition and crime. It was characteristic of the Pharisees that "they said, and did not." (Matt. xxiii. 2.) It is, moreover, important to bear in mind that the party in power, by whom the death of Jesus was actually planned and effected, was that of the Sadducees, though the Pharisees were acting in concert with them. (John xi. 49–53, and 57; Acts iv. 1; v. 17.) The Sadducees rejected the oral tradition on which the Pharisees built their religious system, though in their interpretation of the written law they were sometimes more strict than the Pharisees themselves, and also more severe in their treatment of offenders.

The day of the week on which the Crucifixion took place being fixed—Friday, the day before the Jewish Sabbath—astronomical calculations prove that Friday, April 7th, in A.D. 30, was not Nisan 14th, but Nisan 15th. The day of this greatest of events appears therefore to be ascertained beyond reasonable doubt. It was FRIDAY, 15th NISAN, and 7th APRIL, A.D. 30.

The ritual of the PASCHAL SUPPER was as follows: When all were arranged at ease around the table, the first cup of wine was poured out, mingled with water, both for refreshment and wholesomeness, and to guard against any danger of intoxication, since each person was expected to drink four cups during the evening. The father of the family, or president of the company, pronounced a blessing (*i.e.* thanksgiving) for the wine and for the festival. Hands were washed with an appropriate blessing. At this point we may suppose our Lord rose from the table, and astonished His disciples by washing their feet. (John xiii. 3–17.) Bitter herbs, such as lettuces, were brought and eaten, dipped in sour sauce. Then cakes of unleavened bread, the roasted paschal lamb, with the *chagigah*, if there were one, and the thick sauce (made of dates, raisins, almonds, etc., with vinegar) called "charoseth." A second cup of wine was mingled; and in answer to the appointed question (Ex. xii. 26), the father or president explained the meaning of the paschal sacrifice, the unleavened bread, and the bitter herbs, quoting also Deut. xxvi. 5–11. Part of the Hallel, or hymn of praise, was then sung, viz. Ps. cxiii., cxiv. Then the president, having again washed his hands, placed one cake of bread on another, broke it, and pronounced a blessing. It was eaten, dipped in charoseth, with bitter herbs. This explains "the sop" given to Judas. A blessing was in like manner pronounced over the lamb. Each one ate at his pleasure, but a mouthful of lamb must be the last thing eaten. The third cup was then mingled, over which the blessing or thanksgiving for the meal was pronounced, and which was therefore called "the cup of blessing." (Comp. 1 Cor. x. 16; xi. 25.) The remainder of the Hallel, viz. Ps. cxv.–cxviii., was sung over the fourth cup. This is "the hymn" referred to in Matt. xxvi. 30. (Pesachim, ch. x.)

"The cup" referred to in Luke xxii. 17 is doubtless the "first cup," which introduced the meal. Our Lord's words have been understood as implying that He did not Himself partake of it. This appears extremely improbable, and at variance with ver. 15, 16; and the Greek word, as Dean Alford points out, favours the belief that He drank first, according to custom. "The cup after supper" (Luke xxii. 20; comp. 1 Cor. xi. 25) was evidently the *third* cup of the prescribed ritual—"the cup of blessing." Of this cup, which He constituted the symbol of His own sacrifice, we cannot suppose our Lord to have partaken. (See Matt. xxvi. 29; Mark xiv. 25.) Of the fourth cup, as well as of the second, the brief Gospel narrative takes no notice; nor can we be certain that our Lord observed every minute detail of the traditional ritual.

It is thus evident that the institution of THE LORD'S SUPPER (1 Cor. xi. 20)—the consecration of "the bread which we break," and "the cup of blessing which we bless" (1 Cor. x. 16), as the perishing yet imperishable memorials of "the body and blood of the Lord" (xi. 27)—was not a separate observance, a sort of after-meal following the paschal supper, but an integral part of that supper. It was "as they did eat"—while the meal was in progress—that the Lord gave thanks and broke the bread (Matt. xxvi. 21; Mark xiv. 22). This act must not be confounded with the customary "bread-breaking," already noticed, when the blessing *followed* the breaking. It would at once arrest the disciples' attention as something special and unprecedented, but still an integral part of the paschal meal. In like manner, it was "the cup after supper"—the customary third cup, one of the most important parts of the whole observance—of which Jesus said, "This cup is the new covenant in My blood, . . . shed for many for the remission of sins." (Luke xxii. 20; Matt. xxvi. 28.) Any notion of sacerdotal consecration was utterly foreign to the whole transaction, and could never have occurred to the mind of a single disciple. The Lord was acting not as a priest, but as the father of the family, or president of the company. The Apostles could but dimly understand the meaning of their Master's words at the time, because His body was not yet "broken" nor His blood "shed." But what we may be absolutely certain of is, that neither then nor subsequently could the insane imagination enter their minds, that as He broke the bread and took the cup, He was literally holding in His hands His own crucified and glorified body, and His own blood about to be shed on the cross, but every drop of which was as yet in His veins. Yet unless this was so, the words of institution afford no shadow of foundation for the dogma of Transubstantiation. It is urged that this is the literal sense of the words. But if by "literal sense" be intended a meaning—or absence of meaning—which they could not possibly convey to those who heard them, then it is evident that all talk about "*literal meaning*" is beside the mark. What we are always first concerned with, is the *real* meaning of a speaker's words; whether literal or figurative is a secondary matter.

The traitor had gone out on his hideous errand into the lonely streets, fully possessed now by that spirit of evil which was to hurry him before sunrise from crime to despair, and from despair to self-murder. As yet, perhaps, the hush lay unbroken over the Holy City, the air of which would soon be filled with the voice of the psalmody from the hundreds of thousands crowded within its walls. Relieved of that hateful presence, the Saviour began to unburden His heart, and to draw closer to Himself than ever before the hearts of the chosen few, whose weakness He knew so much better than they themselves, yet whom He knew to be true, though weak. It is scarcely too much to say, that the FAREWELL DISCOURSE recorded in the 14th, 15th, and 16th chapters of St. John, and THE PRAYER in the 17th, are to the rest of the New Testament what the Holy of Holies was to the rest of the Temple, so deeply do they lead us into communion with Him in whom "dwelleth the fulness of the Godhead bodily."

The words (xiv. 31) "*Arise, let us go hence,*" seem to indicate the going forth from the "guest-chamber," after the singing of the Hallel. The rest of the discourse (chap. xv., xvi.) was therefore probably spoken and the prayer (chap. xvii.) offered in the open air, in the court-yard of the house. The similitude of the Vine and its branches may have been suggested from a vine trained, according to custom, by the house on a trellis. The dead wood having been cut away at an earlier pruning, the luxuriant young shoots require at this season a second pruning.

It can scarcely have been less than three hours after sunset when "Jesus went forth with His disciples over the brook Kedron." (John xviii. 1, 2; Matt. xxvi. 30–36; Mark xiv. 26–32; Luke xxii. 39.) The full moon was more than three hours high, pouring her light (unless the sky was clouded, which at full moon is rare) on the stupendous eastern and southern walls and cloisters of the Temple enclosures, and on the path down into the valley; but the lower slopes of Olivet lay in shadow. Possibly the mention of "lanterns and torches" (John xviii. 3) intimates that the night was dark and stormy, as well as cold (ver. 18), though it is not inconsistent with moonlight, since the trees would cast dark shadows, and lights might be needed for dark passages and gateways. Stormy weather is not infrequent at Jerusalem about this season, which is included in the time of the "latter rains."

The AGONY IN GETHSEMANE is one of those passages in our Saviour's life—the Temptation being the other —which could be known only in one of two ways— from His own lips, or by direct supernatural revelation. The distance to which for privacy He withdrew (Luke xxii. 41) might possibly allow the sound of His voice to be heard in the still night air, but certainly not His words. Moreover, the three disciples were asleep. We have no reason to suppose that the "Angel from heaven" (ver. 43) was visible to any one but Jesus. No human eye witnessed those "great drops of blood falling down to the ground" (ver. 44) which His intense agony forced out,—the portent, but for the miraculous succour, of sudden death. After this awful season had passed we see our Lord exhibiting the most perfect calmness, majestic self-restraint, and unshaken fortitude, to the time of

His death. (Matt. xxvi. 36–46; Mark xiv. 33–42; Luke xxii. 40–46. Comp. Heb. v. 7.)

The BETRAYAL AND ARREST OF JESUS are related by all four Evangelists. We may suppose that at least another hour of the night was spent, and that it wanted less than two hours to midnight, when the stillness was broken by the tramp of footsteps and the confused noise of an approaching multitude, led, as it soon appeared, by the traitor. The first two Gospels speak of "a great multitude with swords and staves, from the chief priests and elders." The peculiar words used by St. John, rendered "band" and "captain" ("*speira*," a "cohort;" comp. Matt. xxvii. 27; "*chiliarchos*," more properly "colonel"), have been understood to imply that the priests had obtained a Roman guard from Pilate. Perhaps this is one of the over-refinements of minute criticism. The Levites who formed the Temple guard were trained soldiers (2 Chron. xxiii. 7, 9, 10, 14); and it is on the face of it extremely improbable that such an application would be made, as well as difficult to reconcile with the subsequent account. St. John's narrative supplies several particulars omitted in the three earlier Gospels, and is strongly stamped with the tokens of having been written by an eye-witness. He alone mentions that it was Peter who drew his sword in defence of his Master, and gives the name of the high-priest's servant on whom Jesus wrought His LAST MIRACLE of healing. (Matt. xxvi. 47–56; Mark xiv. 43–52; Luke xxii. 47–53; John xviii. 3–12.)

The first three Gospels agree in recording that JESUS was taken to THE PALACE OF CAIAPHAS, THE HIGH-PRIEST. Matthew alone names him; Luke says, "Into the high-priest's house." Here the members of the Sanhedrin had previously met (Matt. xxvi. 3), and here they speedily assembled (the Greek word does not require to be rendered "*were assembled*" as in A. V.), not, indeed, for a legal meeting, which neither the time nor the place allowed, but to enjoy their triumph in having their dreaded enemy helpless, as it seemed, and friendless in their grasp, and to prepare, by questioning Him and gathering hostile testimony, for His formal condemnation. St. John alone, in his fuller account, informs us that Jesus was conducted "to Annas first, for he was father-in-law to Caiaphas" (xviii. 13); and that Annas sent Him to Caiaphas (ver. 24). Annas, or Hanan (Josephus calls him Ananus), was very possibly a more influential person than Caiaphas himself. He had been high-priest for a considerable number of years, until deposed by the fourth Roman Governor, Pilate's predecessor. He lived to see five of his sons hold the office, besides his son-in-law, Joseph Caiaphas (Jos. *Ant.* xviii. 2: 2; xx. 9: 1). The title of high-priest is given him by St. Luke (iii. 2; Acts iv. 6). It is most probable that he was *Sagan*, or chief ruler of the priests. Some writers assume that he was *Nasi*, or president of the Sanhedrin. This is an error, for the president of the Sanhedrin was the famous Gamaliel, son of the great Hillel, in whose family the office of Nasi continued for many generations. But it is not improbable he may have been vice-president ("*Ab Beth-din*," "father of the court"). As we find no mention of Gamaliel, we may infer that he and other leading Pharisees, like Joseph of Arimathea and Nicodemus (Luke xxiii. 50, 51; John xix. 38, 39), held aloof from these violent and lawless proceedings, leaving the whole management in the hands of Annas, Caiaphas, and their fellow Sadducees.

St. John expressly calls Caiaphas the high-priest in verses 13, 24. It is therefore natural to suppose that it is Caiaphas, and no one else, who is referred to in the intervening verses (15, 16, 19, 22), and, indeed, very unnatural to suppose anything else. The supposition that these intervening verses describe a preliminary trial before Annas, not only introduces confusion and even contradiction into St. John's narrative, but involves hopeless discrepancy in the accounts of Peter's denial. The only reason for this confusing supposition lies in the fact, that verse 24 stands where it does instead of immediately following verse 14; together with the view that, in grammatical strictness, instead of "*Now Annas had sent*," we ought to translate "*Annas therefore sent*." But there is really no difficulty in understanding that St. John, having been led by the mention of Caiaphas to refer back to what he has formerly told us (xi. 49–52), omits to state that Annas sent Jesus on to the high-priest, and therefore adds this explanation at verse 24. And with reference to the tense, there is ample evidence of the very free use of the Greek aorist or indefinite tense; and a minute grammatical refinement of this sort cannot withstand the plain sense of a whole passage. We are therefore fully justified in taking John xviii. 19–23 as parallel with the accounts of the midnight trial before Caiaphas and the members of the Sanhedrin, recorded in the first two Gospels. (Matt. xxvi. 57–66; Mark xiv. 55–64.)

Simon Peter is represented throughout the Gospels as confessedly the foremost man among the band of apostles; he appears in the Acts—the second part of Luke's Gospel—as the first great preacher of the Christian Church, and he was the close friend of the Evangelist John. It is, therefore, a most striking example of the faithfulness of the writers, that all four Gospels fully record the affecting and humiliating story of what is commonly and expressively spoken of as "PETER'S FALL." The variations are such as we expect from different narrators relating truly what they witnessed or learned from eye-witnesses. Bearing in mind the structure of a large Eastern house, we can easily follow the narrative. The door and passage from the street admit to a court or quadrangle, on the opposite side of which is the principal hall or reception room, open in front to the court. Behind is an inner court, and in a large mansion a third, into which the private rooms open, where no stranger may intrude. Peter, being admitted to the palace through the intervention of "another disciple," who was known to the high-priest (John xviii. 16)—doubtless John—found himself in the quadrangle crowded with servants and officers, gathered round a fire in the centre of the court. Peter was able at first to sit down unnoticed, waiting "to see the end;" his grief, terror, and perplexity perhaps not unmixed with feelings of indignation and resentment that his brave attempt to defend his Master single-handed had drawn on him only severe rebuke. John describes him and the rest as standing, which creates no difficulty: if there were a few benches, they would stand and sit by turns. As the ruddy glow fell on his face, the portress who had admitted him at John's request, chancing to come near the fire, pointed him out as a disciple of Jesus. Peter "denied before them all," protesting that he did not know what she meant. He withdrew into the shelter of the passage leading into the street (" the porch "). The crowing of a cock smote on his ear and heart; but he had now committed himself too far to retract, or possibly he was too much absorbed in the tumult of feeling to remember his Lord's warning. (Mark only notices this first cock-crowing.) We are not expressly told that he returned from the porch, but Mark,.in speaking of "them that stood by" (xiv. 69), distinctly implies this, while Matthew's brief account in no way contradicts it. The second accusation was urged by many voices ("another [maid]," Matt.; "the maid," Mark; "another [man]," Luke; "they," John). Peter's second denial was correspondingly vehement. "About an hour" elapsed, and Peter perhaps thought himself safe from further notice, when he found himself confronted with

THE SUFFERINGS OF CHRIST. 145

a kinsman of Malchus, who had actually seen him, sword in hand, in the garden. A chorus of bystanders appealed to Peter's north-country brogue as clear evidence that he was a follower of the Prophet of Galilee. The unhappy disciple lost all self-control, and emphasized with curses his repeated denials. The third hour after midnight was now wearing away. "The second time the cock crew." At the same moment "the Lord turned and looked upon Peter." St. Mark's statement (ver. 66), that Peter was "*beneath*" in the palace court, implying that the principal room, though open to the court, was raised above it, forbids the supposition that Peter was a spectator of what was going on before Caiaphas, or that our Lord could have looked upon Peter while yet standing before that infamous tribunal. We may therefore infer that by this time the council had adjourned until daybreak, and that Jesus had been brought down to endure the scoffs and outrages of the servants and soldiers in the courtyard. As He was rudely led near the spot where His faithless disciple was standing, that look was suddenly turned on Peter, the mingled majesty, tenderness, sorrow, and loving yet awful rebuke of which we may venture silently to imagine. The warning, so incredible when uttered, but which had been fulfilled to the letter, rushed back into Peter's mind, and with it how much beside! Overwhelmed with grief and shame, he hurried out bitterly weeping. The special message to Peter after the resurrection (Mark xvi. 7), and separate appearance of the risen Lord to him (Luke xxiv. 34; 1 Cor. xv. 5) we may well believe to have been needful, in order to assure him that he was no outcast, but still loved and freely forgiven. (Matt. xxvi. 58, 69–75; Mark xiv. 54, 66–72; Luke xxii. 54–62; John xviii. 15–18.)

The meeting of the Sanhedrin in the house of Caiaphas was irregular and informal: first, because it was against their rule to try a capital cause by night; second, because their proper place of meeting was in the Temple. It was also contrary to rule to pass judgment on a feast day; but this rule seems to have been set aside by the emergency of the occasion. The Talmud states that forty years before the destruction of the Temple the Sanhedrin removed its sessions from the hall Gazith, its proper meeting-place, to certain outbuildings of the Temple (called "the sheds" or "shops"), and afterwards away from the Temple altogether; and that at the same date "judgment of capital crimes was taken from Israel." Whether this was before or after the time of our Lord's death is uncertain. Lightfoot (on John xviii. 31) elaborately argues from various Rabbinical statements that the Jewish rulers were not deprived of the power of life and death by any formal act of the Roman Government, but that in consequence of the frightful multiplication of murders and other crimes, the Sanhedrin, not daring to execute justice, abandoned its claim to try capital cases. The lesser Sanhedrins lost their power at the same time. The hall Gazith opened by one entrance into the *Chel*, or consecrated space between the wall of the Temple courts and the court of the Gentiles, and by another entrance into the court of the priests. We have, I think, an indication that the morning sitting of the council was in the hall Gazith, in what is recorded of the traitor JUDAS, who when Jesus was condemned flung down the price of his treachery "in the Temple" (Matt. xxvii. 3–10). The word here used for Temple (*naos*, as in xxiii. 16 ; xxvi. 61; xxvii. 40–51) is applicable only to the innermost building, *i.e.*, the Holy Place and the Holy of Holies, a different word (*hieron*) being used in such passages as Matt. xxvi. 55; Luke ii. 37, etc. Into the Holy Place none but a priest dared enter. The obvious inference is, that Judas was a priest. Entering, as I conjecture, the hall

Gazith by the outer door, and being treated with cold scorn by "the chief priests and elders," the unhappy wretch, in the fury of his despair, passed by the inner door into the priests' court, mounted the steps of the sanctuary, and flung down "the price of blood" upon the sacred floor.

At break of day A MEETING OF THE SANHEDRIN was convened, which might bear some semblance of legal authority. Jesus was arraigned, and failing all consistent witness on which to found a demand to the Roman Governor for His death, His foes (in defiance of their own rules) endeavoured to force from Him some confession on which to found their sentence. If we are to believe the Talmud, the one fatal weakness of the Sanhedrin was its excessive mildness towards criminals, and its abhorrence of condemning an Israelite to death. If these traditions deserve any credence, the men who would have acted in the spirit they describe—the Gamaliels, Josephs, Nicodemuses—were absent. The stern, politic, worldly-minded Sadducees scorned alike tradition and clemency. Jesus declined to repeat the declaration which, when adjured by Caiaphas, He had made the night before, that He was "THE CHRIST, THE SON OF GOD," which of course involved His claim to be King of Israel. But when asked if He was THE SON OF GOD, He replied in the well-understood form of assent—"*Ye say that I am.*" Immediately He was condemned by acclamation, "and the whole multitude of them arose, and LED HIM TO PILATE." (Luke xxii. 66–71; xxiii. 1; Matt. xxvii. 1, 2; Mark xv. 1; John xviii. 28.)

The PRÆTORIUM, as the residence for the time being of the Roman Governor was called,[1] was in all proba-

---

[1] The proper title of the Governor of Judæa (which was included in the province of Syria) was "Procurator"—"Steward" or "Commissioner"; but he had the power of "Imperial Lieutenant," involving prætorian rank. (See Smith's *Dict. of Rom. and Greek Ant.*, Art. "Provincia";

bility the Citadel or Castle called Antonia, situate at the north-west corner of the Temple area, and commanding the Temple by means of a passage to the cloisters. Combining the strength of a fortress with the magnificence of a palace, and forming the key to the possession of Jerusalem, it would be the natural residence of the Roman Governor when at Jerusalem. This view is confirmed by St. Mark's statement (xv. 16) that the soldiers called " the whole band " together —implying that the whole garrison was within call.

Along that very passage then, most probably, through which His servant Paul was led nearly thirty years afterwards (Acts xxi. 31–35; xxiii. 10), the rejected King of Israel was hurried by the infuriated priests, thirsting for His blood, yet not daring themselves to shed it. They demanded an immediate audience of the governor; and Pontius Pilate, knowing that their customs forbade their entering the citadel, came out to meet them. "It was early." The Greek word here and elsewhere used may signify, according to circumstances, either before sunrise or between sunrise and noon. Sunrise at Jerusalem on the 6th April is between ten minutes and a quarter before six. The Sanhedrin would have been able to meet soon after five. The condemnation of Jesus was a foregone conclusion, and we may be certain that they lost no time in seeking to make Pilate the executioner of their murderous purpose. They seem at first to have imagined that the fear of popular tumult would induce the Roman Governor to order the execution of Jesus on their bare assertion that He was "a malefactor." Pilate, however, was not without some sense both of

Con. and Howson, vol. i. pp. 27, 155.) Concerning the Castle Antonia or Baris (supposed to be referred to Nehemiah ii. 8), and the two palaces—one built by Herod the Great, the other by the Maccabees—see *Handbook to Bible*, pp. 347, 354, 355, 385; Jos. *Ant.*, xviii. 4: 3; *Wars*, i. 21: 1: v. 5: 8; 4: 4; *Ant.*, xx. 8: 11; *Wars*, ii. 16: 8.

dignity and of justice, and replied that if they wanted a prisoner put to death without trial, they must both pass sentence and execute it. Their reply (the exact meaning of which is disputed; see p. 146) was to the effect that they could not lawfully inflict capital punishment. (John xviii. 29–32; Luke xxiii. 2.) They added that Jesus had publicly taught sedition, "forbidding to give tribute to Cæsar, saying that He Himself is Christ a King." (Luke xxiii. 2. N.B.—This accusation, though not expressly noticed by St. John, is *implied* in xviii. 33–35.)

Pilate, who could scarcely be without some previous knowledge of Jesus, saw that he had a case of no ordinary difficulty to deal with. Jesus, alike before the Sanhedrin, before Herod, and before Pilate, maintained absolute silence when His replying to a question or an accusation would have put Him in the position of standing on His defence, and thus recognizing the right of any tribunal to arraign Him. But as He had answered the high-priest's question whether He was the Son of God, so now He replied to Pilate's question whether He was the King of the Jews. The character of His answer increased Pilate's perplexity, and convinced him that the enemies of Jesus were seeking, not justice, but vengeance. He therefore went out to the accusers, and declared that he found no reason to comply with their demand. (John xviii. 33–38; Luke xxiii. 3, 4; Matt. xxvii. 11; Mark xv. 2.)

The priests were stirred to increased violence by the fear that the victim might after all escape. Their reference to Galilee as the birthplace of the seditious teaching of which they accused Jesus, suggested to Pilate a way out of the difficulty by throwing the responsibility on Herod Antipas, who had come to Jerusalem for the festival, and who may have been occupying either his father's splendid palace or the palace built by the Maccabees. To Herod accordingly Jesus was forthwith sent. The Tetrarch, whose coarse and cruel mind was not without gleams of right impulse (Mark vi. 20), seems to have regarded Jesus, whom he had formerly conjectured to be John the Baptist risen from the dead, as a religious enthusiast whose regal claims were best extinguished by ridicule. Irritated at the silence of Jesus, and disappointed in his hope of seeing Him perform a miracle, he delivered Him to his guards to be made sport of, and sent Him back to Pilate clothed in mockery with a brilliant robe. (Luke xxiii. 6-12.)[1] This appears to be the mocking referred to by St. John (xix. 2, 3), though he may also refer to that subsequently inflicted by Pilate's soldiers.

Meantime a murmur was rising among the crowd that the Roman Governor, according to a singular custom noticed in all the Gospels, should release a prisoner in honour of the feast. (Mark xv. 8.) Pilate flattered himself that he saw a fresh way of escape. Again he declared Jesus guiltless, and appealed to Herod's judgment in confirmation of his own. He

---

[1] The word means "shining," "splendid," and may therefore be applied to white raiment (Rev. xv. 6), but it does not *mean* "white." In James ii. 2, 3, it is translated "goodly," "gay." There is therefore no reason why we should not understand it of the same robe which Matthew calls "scarlet," and Mark and John "purple." Dean Alford (on Luke xxiii. 12) writes as if St. John was ignorant of the sending of Jesus by Pilate to Herod,—which, of course, must imply that it never happened. "Obviously," he says, "nothing was further from the mind of the Evangelist." We might as justly infer from Ex. ii. 1, 2, that nothing was further from the mind of Moses than that he had a brother and sister older than himself. The *absolute* way in which the inspired writers omit what they do not see fit distinctly to narrate, is one great secret of the terseness, force, and brilliancy of Scripture narratives; and if not a proof of inspiration, is at least a very remarkable feature of the historical Scriptures. It is worth noting that Luke alone records the fact that our Lord was sent to Herod, but for which record the reference in Acts iv. 27 would be unintelligible.

THE SUFFERINGS OF CHRIST.

offered, as a concession to the malice of the priests, to scourge Jesus, and then to release Him, proposing as an alternative name that of a notorious criminal, whom he evidently hoped they would reject. The relentless answer was, "Not this man, but Barabbas." (Matt. xxvii. 15-18; Mark xv. 6-11; Luke xxiii. 13-19; John xviii. 39, 40.)

That the scourging inflicted by Pilate's order was not the flogging with rods which St. Paul thrice suffered (2 Cor. xi. 25; Acts xvi. 22; and Alf.'s Note), but the severer and more degrading torture of the lash, is clear from the Greek words employed by the Evangelists. This appears to have been the customary preliminary to crucifixion. (Jos., *Wars*, ii. 14: 9.) There is no sufficient evidence, however, that that most horrible form of scourge was employed, under the torture of which slaves and criminals sometimes died. (*Dict. of Ant.*, Art. "Flagellum;" Farrar, vol. ii. pp. 379, 380; Geikie, vol. ii. p. 547.) The scourging was probably the courtyard of the Castle. St. John distinctly places it before Pilate's renewed refusal to crucify Jesus (xix. 1, ff.). It has therefore been inferred from Matt. xxvii. 26; Mark xv. 15, that Jesus was *a second time* scourged, after Pilate's final sentence. But this is almost incredible, and is by no means necessarily implied, the phrase (strictly translated) "*having scourged Him*" simply asserting that this customary infliction was not omitted.

Pilate, cherishing a lingering hope that this punishment (confessedly unmerited) might appease the rage and hatred of the accusers of Jesus, brought Him forth (perhaps on the steps of the Castle, Acts xxi. 40), "wearing the crown of thorns and the purple robe." "BEHOLD THE MAN!" he said; as much as to ask, "Is it not enough?" The reply was the remorseless shout, "Crucify! Crucify!" Stern and cruel as he could show himself under provocation (comp. Jos., *Ant.* xviii. 3: 2; 4: 1, 2), the Roman shrank from becoming an accomplice in cold blood in a judicial murder. He again bitterly told the Jewish rulers that if nothing but the blood of Jesus would satisfy them, they might crucify Him themselves. Their reply added to the awe which from the first the person of Jesus had inspired in Pilate, and which was doubtless increased by the singular message he had received from his wife. (Matt. xxvii. 19.) Once more he retired within the Castle, and called Jesus before him. Bleeding from the scourge, after some eight hours of mental and bodily anguish almost inconceivable, Jesus replied to Pilate with as calm majesty as though He had been seated on the judgment seat, and Pilate the prisoner upon his trial. In real truth—so different from outward seeming—it was so. (John xix. 1–11.)

For the last time Pilate renewed his attempt to turn the Jewish rulers from their purpose. He was met by an argument before which his courage quailed. If he spared one who claimed the throne of Israel, his own loyalty to Cæsar would be called in question. Pilate was vanquished. He had fought for justice and mercy as strenuously as perhaps any man could do with whom conscience is motive only, not law. He was not prepared to save the life of Jesus at the cost of his own. He took his seat upon the "curule chair" (or rather "stool"), as the seat of magistrates exercising the power of life and death was called (in Greek "*bema;*" Acts xviii. 12; xxv. 10; Rom. xiv. 10).[1] For

[1] St. John says, "*In a place called the Pavement, but in Hebrew Gabbatha.*" The latter word (essentially the same with "*Gibbethon*," 1 Kings xv. 27) is not given as an exact translation of the Greek word rendered "Pavement," but as the name by which the Jews called the place where Pilate sat in judgment. It was probably a raised terrace, perhaps of marble, in front of the Castle. Since the *place*, not the *pavement*, is intended, the accounts quoted by various writers of the *movable pavement* which Julius Cæsar carried with him on his journeys have no application; nor can there be any reference here to the pavement of the Temple.

THE SUFFERINGS OF CHRIST. 153

the last time the Man of Sorrows was led forth by the Roman guards in view of the dense and excited multitude, which by this time probably filled the whole area between the Castle and the Temple. Pilate's final appeal seems rather to have been made to the people than to the priests alone. "BEHOLD YOUR KING!... Shall I crucify your King?" The reply of the chief priests was the death-knell of Israel's national life: "We have no king but Cæsar!" (John xix. 12-15.) Priests and people joined in the cry that Pilate should release Barabbas and crucify Jesus. (Matt. xxvii. 20-23; Mark xv. 12-14; Luke xxiii. 16-23.) St. Matthew relates the solemn symbolic act by which Pilate sought to divest himself of responsibility for the crime from which he vainly sought to deter the Jews. Washing his hands before all the people, he pronounced the most extraordinary preface to a death sentence ever heard from a judgment-seat—"*I am innocent of the blood of this just person; see ye to it.*" The chorus of the popular voice ratified the demand of their priestly leaders. "Then answered all the people, and said, His blood be on us, and on our children." (Matt. xxvii. 24, 25.)

"And so Pilate, willing to content the people, released BARABBAS unto them, and delivered JESUS, when he had scourged Him, TO BE CRUCIFIED." (Mark xv. 15-20; Matt. xxvii. 26-31; Luke xxiii. 24, 25; John xix. 16.)

The soldiers led Jesus within the courtyard of the Castle, and "the whole cohort" joined in repeating the coarse and cruel mockery of which Herod's soldiers had set the example. (Matt. xxvii. 27-31; Mark xv. 16-20.) At length the second act of this great tragedy was over. "And they took Jesus, and led Him away; and He bearing His cross went forth." (John xix. 16, 17). It was customary for one condemned to crucifixion to carry his cross, or a part of it; but the first three Gospels record the name of SIMON OF CYRENE as having been compelled to bear the cross after Jesus. The traditional explanation is reasonable, that after the strain and exhaustion of so many hours of mental and bodily anguish our Lord's bodily strength was no longer equal to the burden, and He sank under it. (Matt. xxviii. 32; Mark xv. 21; Luke xxiii. 26.)

As we "consider Him that endured such contradiction of sinners against Himself," we must not leave out of sight the amazing self-control with which He restrained that power before which His foes would have been as chaff before the tempest. (Psa. i. 4; ii. 12.) The voice which had stilled the wind and waves could have loosed the lightning and earthquake, blinded every hostile eye and withered every arm lifted against Him. But He was led "as a lamb to the slaughter." (Isa. liii. 7; Phil. ii. 8.) As we review the accumulated blasphemy, injustice, ingratitude, outrage, cruelty, of those long hours, we are ready to think that—so far as the sufferings men could inflict were concerned— the cross itself could have nothing worse in store.

St. John says, "*It was about the sixth hour,*" when Pilate made his last appeal to the Jews, and sentenced Jesus to the cross. St. Mark, describing the execution of the sentence, says, "*It was the third hour, and they crucified Him.*" This discrepancy was attempted to be solved as early as the time of Eusebius, by supposing "*sixth*" to be a mere error of copyists for "*third.*" This supposition, in the face of the actual state of the text, has not found favour with modern editors. The explanation adopted by Townson, Greswell, and Wieseler has been defended with great learning and earnestness by McClellan (*Four Gospels*, pp. 737–743), viz., that as the Romans, although employing the ordinary reckoning of the day from sunrise to sunset, had also a civil day from midnight to midnight, they divided this day into twenty-four hours, as we do; and that the Evangelist uses this reckoning. Thus by "the sixth hour" would be meant, not noon, but six a.m. The fatal objection to this explanation is not the doubtfulness of the arguments in its favour, but the impossibility of making it fit with the facts. The Sanhedrin met at daybreak, soon after five a.m. Orientals are not accustomed to the rapid dispatch of business familiar to ourselves. Twenty minutes is a short time to allow from their assembling to their rising. Another ten or fifteen minutes would elapse in conveying their Prisoner to the front of the Castle and demanding an audience of the Governor. By the time Pilate came out to them the sun had probably already risen. By the time he had privately conversed with Jesus, held his second interview with the priests, and come to the resolution to send Jesus to Herod, the sixth hour from midnight must have been passed. We cannot reckon less than twenty minutes for the descent into the Tyropœan valley and ascent to Herod's palace on Mount Zion, and the same for returning. The interview with Herod, and the mockery by his soldiers, cannot be supposed to have occupied less than half an hour. It would thus, at the earliest, be between seven and eight a.m. when Jesus again stood before Pilate. Then followed Pilate's offer to release Jesus; then the scourging, after which He was brought out to the people, wearing the crown of thorns; another private interview within the Prætorium; and a final attempt to turn the Jews from their purpose, before Pilate took his seat to pass sentence. All this implies a considerable interval of time, and agrees well with Mark's statement that "it was the third hour," or about nine a.m., when the place of crucifixion was reached. It would not be extravagant even to allow a couple of hours longer for these transactions; and in that case the phrase "*about the sixth hour*" might be taken as merely meaning "it was now drawing near mid-day." We must then suppose a copyist's error in the second Gospel, not the fourth. But that

156 OUTLINES OF THE LIFE OF CHRIST.

all these events could have been transacted in the interval of less than one hour, between daybreak and six a.m., is an impossibility, which no amount of erudition can make possible. We seem, therefore, shut up to Dean Alford's conclusion, that "we must certainly suppose, as did Eusebius, Theophylact, and Severus, that there has been some very early erratum in our copies."

Combining, therefore, the facts narrated by the four Evangelists with the express statement of St. Mark, we gather that four hours or more had elapsed since the meeting of the Sanhedrin at daybreak, and that it wanted some three hours of noon when the rejected King of Israel reached "Golgotha"—doubtless the accustomed place of public executions.[1] St. Luke (xxiii. 27–32) records the remarkable prophecy uttered by our Lord, showing that His self-possession and majestic bearing were unabated by His sufferings; he also mentions that the two criminals, whom all the Gospels state to have been crucified at His side, were "led with Him." On arriving at the spot, as the first two Gospels tell us (Matt. xxvii. 34; Mark xv. 23), a stupefying cup was offered to Him, containing myrrh dissolved in wine—a customary gift from some wealthy and compassionate women of Jerusalem to criminals condemned to the cross (Lightfoot). Matthew employs the terms "*vinegar*" and "*gall*" (which might be used for any bitter herb; see Robinson's Lex.), to indicate the fulfilment of prophecy (Psa. lxix. 21). The Sufferer having been stripped and nailed to the cross, a writing was by Pilate's

[1] Matthew, Mark, and John give the Hebrew name, which they explain "*the place of a skull.*" Luke simply uses the Greek word for "*skull*," latinized in our translation into "*Calvary.*" The place has been, with high probability if not certainty, identified with the spot known as "the place of stoning," north of Jerusalem, to which the name "Mount" (though not applied in Scripture) is not wholly inapplicable. See *Tent Work*, vol. i. pp. 371–376.

THE SUFFERINGS OF CHRIST.

order fixed above His head, in three languages, that it might be read by the native Jews, the foreign Jews, of whom great numbers attended the feast, and the Roman soldiers. In each language He was declared to be "THE KING OF THE JEWS." St. John (xix. 20–22) records Pilate's stern refusal to alter this inscription.

The fiendish spirit of mockery which burst forth with new fury at the foot of the cross, as before in the high-priest's palace, the palace of Herod, and the Prætorium, while it reveals in hateful colours the character of the people and of the times, is vividly suggestive of more than human malice, recalling our Lord's references to "*the power of darkness.*" (Luke xxii. 53; John xiv. 30.) If we are to take the words of the first two Gospels as strictly literal (which perhaps is unnecessary), both the malefactors at first joined in these taunts. St. Luke, who alone relates the prayer of Jesus for His murderers (xxiii. 34), also tells how the conscience of one of these guilty men, as he watched the patient majesty of the Divine Sufferer, was pierced, and his heart inspired with a faith alike unique and marvellous; and how to him was granted the transcendent honour of being the Saviour's comforter during those dark hours, and the trophy, when He seemed unable to save Himself, of His power to save (ver. 39–43). Besides these two UTTERANCES ON THE CROSS, five others are recorded in the Gospels, SEVEN in all; namely, the words in which Jesus commended His mother to the care of His beloved disciple (John xix. 25-27); the prayer from Psalm xxii. 1 (Matt. xxvii. 46; Mark xv. 34); the cry of thirst (John ver. 21-30; *implied* in Matt. ver. 48; Mark ver. 36); the cry "*It is finished*" (John ver. 30; comp. Matt. ver. 50; Mark ver. 37); and the dying prayer (Luke ver. 46). The first three Gospels agree in recording the darkness which prevailed from noon till the ninth hour "the hour of prayer" in the

158 OUTLINES OF THE LIFE OF CHRIST.

Temple (Acts iii. 1)—between the slaying of the sacrifice, half an hour after the eighth hour, and the offering of it, half an hour after the ninth (Mishna, Pes. v. 1). They also agree in mentioning the awful portent of the rending of the veil in the Temple, apparently at the moment of our Lord's death. Matthew adds the earthquake, the opening of the graves, and the appearance after Christ's resurrection of saints buried therein. All three record the testimony of the centurion. (Matt. xxvii. 34–56; Mark xv. 22–41; Luke xxiii. 27–49; John xix. 17–24.)

The fourth Gospel relates the method by which the death of the two malefactors was hastened, in order that the bodies might be removed before sunset; and the piercing of the side of Jesus, already dead, when the "*blood and water*"—coagulated blood—which gushed forth furnished proof that His death, which could not naturally have resulted from crucifixion, was not caused by any miraculous intervention, but by His heart having literally burst under the strain of that inconceivable agony.[1] No more affecting and convincing proof can be imagined than this silent testimony, of the reality and intensity of those inward sufferings of which the agony in Gethsemane was the foretaste. We may not presumptuously seek to analyze those sufferings or to separate them from the outward sufferings—the "*body broken for us,*" and "*blood shed for many*"—which He Himself has bidden us to keep in memory. Still we cannot but feel, from our Saviour's own words, both before the cross and upon

---

[1] The evidence, clear and ample, that the immediate cause of our Saviour's death was *a broken heart*, will be found in Dr. Stroud's *Treatise on the Physical Cause of the Death of Christ* (Hamilton and Adams, 1849). His view is of great value as a practical refutation of some unworthy and harmful views. For the details of the punishment of crucifixion the reader may be referred to the *Dict. of Ant.*, and the works of Farrar, Geikie, and Andrews. Terrible as it was, it was incapable of producing so speedy a death.

it, that when He "gave His life a ransom for many," "was wounded for our transgressions," and "His own self bare our sins in His own body on the tree," and when God "made His soul an offering for sin," there was an inconceivably darker and more awful element in His suffering, in relation to Divine law and the Divine will, than they who looked upon the crucifixion could perceive, or than we can fathom. And to this transcendent element is to be added the immense strain of that unswerving purpose and mighty self-restraint by which the Son of God became "obedient unto death," fulfilling His own declaration—"Therefore doth my Father love me, because I lay down my life, that I might take it again. No man taketh it from me, but I lay it down of myself. I have power to lay it down, and I have power to take it again. This commandment have I received of my Father." (John x. 17, 18.)

The Disciples themselves were as ignorant as the myriads of bystanders, Jewish or Heathen, of the true character of that astounding and heartrending spectacle. Only by degrees did the Spirit of truth lead them (John xvi. 13, 14) into the full understanding of the death of Christ for sin. This is clear from comparing the book of Acts with the Epistles. From the outset, the Apostles preached justification by faith in the crucified, risen, glorified Jesus. (See Acts iv. 10–12; xiii. 38, 39.) But the first reference in Acts to the atoning virtue of the death of Christ is in xx. 28. In the two earliest of St. Paul's Epistles occurs but one brief reference—1 Thes. v. 9, 10. But Galations is full of it throughout. (Compare 1 Cor. i. 17, 18, 23; ii. 2; 1 Pet. i. 18, 19; 1 John i. 7; Rev. v. 6, 9.) The "advanced theology" of the New Testament is the doctrine of THE CROSS OF CHRIST.

JERUSALEM

SECTION II.

THE RESURRECTION.

Sunday, April 9th, a.d. 30; Nisan 17th.

THE Shepherd was smitten, and the sheep were scattered. Great crises often bring to light unlooked-for strength, as well as unsuspected weakness. It was not an Apostle or avowed follower of Christ, but a member of the Sanhedrin who had been "a disciple of Jesus, but secretly for fear of the Jews," who "took courage and went to Pilate," startling the Governor with the news that Jesus was already dead, and craving permission to take down the body, and give it honourable burial. His name—Joseph of Arimathæa—is given in all the Gospels. Pilate's feeling concerning Jesus led him at once to grant this request. St. John tells us that another member of the Sanhedrin, Nicodemus, whose secret visit to Jesus, and feeble though well-meant interposition on His behalf, he alone relates (iii. 1; vii. 50), joined with Joseph in providing spices, "*about a hundred pounds weight*," in which the corpse was wrapped. The entombment was hasty, on account of the approach of sunset. Fuller rites were designed when the Sabbath should have passed, by those devoted Galilæan women who had stood by the cross to the last, and watched the burial. The tomb was a rock-hewn one, of that kind used in the later times of Jewish history, in which the corpse was laid in a niche in the side of the tomb, and the entrance to which was closed with a rolling stone. (Matt. xxvi. 57–61; Mark xv. 42–47; Luke xxiii. 50–56; John xix. 38–42.) As to the site of the sepulchre, we are told that it was in a garden, close to the place of crucifixion.

(John xix. 41, 42.) Recent explorations seem to leave no doubt that it was north of the city, where a cemetery exists to this day. (*Tent Work*, vol. i. pp. 361-376; *Handbook to Bible*, pp. 204, 350.)

St. Matthew alone records the precaution taken by the chief priests, together with the Pharisees (whom he has not previously named in connection with the proceedings against Jesus; comp. John xi. 47, 57), to guard against a false report that Jesus was risen from the dead (xxvii. 62-66). His peculiar phrase—" *The next day that followed the day of the preparation*," I take to mean Saturday evening after sunset, when the Sabbath was over. Pilate's answer should be translated imperatively—not " *Ye have a guard*," but " *Take a guard.*" This compliance with their request was of course accompanied with the requisite military orders; and Roman authority and discipline were thus in God's all-watchful providence enlisted as witnesses to the reality of our Lord's resurrection. Matthew also relates the subsequent conduct of the guards, and of the priests, whose words confirm the view that the guards were Roman soldiers (xxviii. 4, 11-15).

" THAT SABBATH DAY was a high day." (John xix. 31.) It was the 16th Nisan, Saturday, April 8th. On it the sheaf of first-fruits, cut with quaint ceremony after sunset of Nisan 15th, was presented with rejoicing in the Temple. (Jos., *Ant.*, iii. 10: 5; *Cyc. Bib. Lit.*, Art. "Passover.") To Caiaphas and his priestly colleagues it was a day of triumph beyond all they could have hoped. Their fears of a popular tumult had proved groundless. Their hated and dreaded enemy was dead and buried, without a hand or voice lifted on His behalf, and they had succeeded in fixing the odium of His death upon the Roman Governor. His followers might linger for awhile as an obscure despised sect, but all fear of their making headway among the people seemed at an end. No less to the disciples themselves it seemed their cause was lost. The Christian Church has seen dark days since, but none so dark as that. No ray of hope cheered their minds "as they mourned and wept." Their Master's repeated predictions of His resurrection remained keyless riddles. When the most devoted of them visited the tomb, it was with no thought but of completing His embalmment. Their reports of the empty sepulchre and of the risen Lord met at first only the incredulity of despair.

The accounts in the four Gospels of the resurrection of Jesus vary, as we expect reports of truthful witnesses to vary. The extreme terseness and brevity of the sacred writers must be borne in mind, together with their habit, already noted, of throwing into strong relief the facts recorded, by absolute silence respecting a multitude of unrecorded details. To infer from this silence either ignorance, or that in any strict sense the different Gospels contain "independent reports," is to forget that they were not written until the facts had been for a dozen or a score of years the constant theme of public teaching and of private converse; and that all the first witnesses were connected by ties of the most intimate companionship and sympathy. The "discrepancies" have been raised into importance partly by the objections of sceptical critics, partly by the ingenuity of harmonists, and partly by the eagerness of some able writers to disparage all attempts at harmony. It is therefore desirable clearly to state the facts which the Evangelists agree in bearing witness to. Manifestly it was not their purpose to furnish a narrative complete in all its details; or even fragmente which, like the pieces of a puzzle, may be fitted together into one whole. Each writer gives a distinct and vivid picture, designed to produce a definite impression, omitting details and qualifications which would destroy the effect of the picture by fixing attention, not on what it contains, but on what it does not contain. To suppose any of the Evangelists ignorant or forgetful of any of the leading facts is to charge him with incompetency or unfaithfulness.

Concerning the following facts, ALL THE NARRATIVES agree. (*a*) The sepulchre was visited early in the morning of the first day of the week by some of the women who had attended Jesus from Galilee, including Mary Magdalene. (*b*) They found the stone rolled away and the tomb empty. (*c*) They saw an angel, or angels, who told them that JESUS was risen. (*d*) The women hastened to carry the tidings to the Apostles, who received them with incredulity. (*e*) Peter and John visited the tomb, but did not see either the Saviour or the angels. (The third and fourth Gospels relate Peter's visit; the fourth states that John was with him.) (*f*) The risen Lord appeared to some of the women. (*g*) He appeared to the Eleven the same evening. (Not referred to by Matthew.) (*h*) Luke adds a separate appearance to Simon Peter (xxiv. 34; comp. 1 Cor. xv. 5), and an appearance to Cleopas and another disciple, to which Mark also refers. (*i*) John alone records an appearance to the Eleven on that day week; likewise a subsequent appearance by the Lake of Galilee. (*j*) Matthew relates a public appearance by solemn appointment in Galilee, to which Mark also alludes (xvi. 7); and which is probably the appearance "to above five hundred brethren," mentioned by St. Paul (1 Cor. xv. 6). (*k*) St. Paul also mentions (ver. 7) an appearance to James, not elsewhere recorded. (*l*) Lastly, Luke (Acts i. 3) intimates that there were repeated and prolonged interviews during the six weeks from the Resurrection to the Ascension, and gives (in his Gospel and in Acts) a double account of the Ascension.

These main facts compose the body of the apostolic "WITNESS OF THE RESURRECTION OF THE LORD JESUS" (Acts iv. 33), which constituted an essential and principal part of their public teaching, and no less of that

THE RESURRECTION. 165

of the Apostle Paul. (1 Cor. xv. 4-14.) The worth of this accordant testimony is no whit diminished by those variations in minute detail to which so great importance has been attached. They are such as would be deemed beneath notice in any ordinary history. Their only claim to regard arises from the value, in records so brief and so precious, of faultless accuracy, and from the bearing which our view of the presence or absence of such accuracy must have on our view of the inspiration under which the Evangelists wrote.

Some of the variations on which sceptical criticism has been expended seem hardly worthy of serious notice: *e.g.*, one Evangelist states that the women *prepared* spices before sunset on Friday evening (Luke xxiii. 56); another, that they *bought* spices after sunset on Saturday. (Mark xvi. 1.) But (not to insist that the translation "*had bought*" is defensible) why should they not be both? Again, a difficulty is found in the varying accounts of the angels, as two or one, sitting or standing, within the sepulchre or outside. It seems to be forgotten that angels are invisible to our natural eyesight, and might therefore appear differently to different persons even at the same time; much more to different persons coming to the spot successively. Again, the variations in the words of the angel or angels—resembling the variations throughout the Gospels in the reports of our Lord's teaching — present no real difficulty. The angel doubtless spoke in Hebrew; and it was no more necessary for the Evangelist to give an exact translation of every word than to record the Hebrew words themselves.

Rationally regarded, the difficulties in harmonizing the four narratives seem to reduce themselves to two questions. (*a*) What relation does John's account of our Lord's appearance to Mary Magdalene bear to the account of His appearance to "the women" in Matt.

xxviii. 9? (*b*) Do the first three Gospels record one vision, or more than one, of angels? In regard to the first question, Mark's statement must be kept in view that "He appeared first to Mary Magdalene."

Without entering on the discussion of the various attempts of commentators and critics either to solve these difficulties or to prove them insoluble, let us follow the record step by step. (1) Of the RESURRECTION itself no account is given. All four Gospels agree that when the women visited the tomb early on Sunday morning they found the stone rolled away and the tomb empty.

(2) As Matthew alone relates the setting of the guard and sealing of the stone, so he alone relates the descent from heaven of an angel who rolled away the stone and sat upon it, the accompanying earthquake, and the terror of the Roman guards. It seems clearly indicated that this took place in preparation for the Lord's resurrection, which no human eye was permitted to behold. The women do not appear to have known anything about the guards, who may be supposed to have recovered from their swoon and departed before any of the women reached the sepulchre. The emphasis in the angel's words, "Fear not YE," was natural from the angel's lips, and equally natural from St. Matthew's pen; but it does not follow that the women understood its allusion to the terror of the soldiers.

(3) Mark tells us that MARY MAGDALENE, MARY the mother of James the Less and of Joses (xv. 40), and SALOME came to the sepulchre "very early in the morning . . . . the sun having risen." (Such is the literal translation. It might be the very minute after sunrise, but the sun had appeared above the horizon.) Matthew mentions the two Marys only. Luke speaks of "the women" who had come from Galilee (xxiii. 49, 55, 56; xxiv. 1); but afterward specifies MARY MAGDALENE MARY the mother of James and JOANNA,

and others with them, as having brought the tidings to the apostles (ver. 9-11). He uses a stronger term to denote the time—"*at deep dawn*,"—*i.e.*, at the earliest daybreak (which on April 9th would be soon after 5 a.m.). With this corresponds ver. 22, where the word rendered "early" means "at daybreak;" and with John's account of Mary Magdalene coming "when it was yet dark." But (as McClellan points out, pp. 521, 526, giving examples: *e.g.*, of the *present tense*, John vi. 19; xi. 20; of *the aorist*, Luke xix. 5; Acts viii. 36) whereas the phrase employed by St. John—"*cometh to*" or "*towards*"—admits the explanation that Mary was *on her way* in the twilight, yet may not have arrived at the tomb before sunrise; St. Luke's phrase—"*came upon*" or "*up to*"—expresses actual arrival. The fact, therefore, seems to have been that some of the women, with the spices they had "prepared," reached the tomb before sunrise, whereas Mary Magdalene with her companions, Mary and Salome, bringing the spices they had "bought," arrived when the first sunbeams were already casting long shadows from the trees of the garden. Here is neither improbability nor inconsistency. The improbability would lie in supposing that all these wealthy matrons were lodging together, either in Jerusalem or in Bethany, or that they could all have reached the spot at once or all before sunrise, having perhaps some of them a distance to travel which over such uneven ground would take not less than half or three-quarters of an hour.

(4) A hasty reader of St. John's account (xx. 1-18) might infer that Mary Magdalene was alone, but her own words—"*We know not where they have laid Him*" —show that she had companions. Her state of mind exactly corresponds with that described by Luke (xxiv. 4)—"*They were much perplexed.*" There would be ample time, while Peter and John hurried to the tomb, and Mary sadly followed, for those who remained

on the spot to see the vision of angels, and to disperse in different directions to carry the tidings. When PETER AND JOHN reached the tomb, they do not appear to have found the women there, or to have seen anything of the angels.

(5) In Luke xxiv. 12, mention is made of Peter only, as though he had gone alone, but ver. 24 speaks of "certain" in the plural. It is touching to see that Peter's deep sin had not estranged from him his old and close friend. We may suppose they were lodging together in the house to which the beloved disciple led the mother of our Lord from the foot of the cross (John xix. 27). The entire silence of all the narratives regarding our Lord's mother is remarkable, and would be almost painful but for the final reference to her in Acts i. 14. It furnishes a caution against drawing inferences from silence.

(6) It seems evident from the prominence given in all the four Gospels to MARY MAGDALENE that she was the first to bring tidings of the empty sepulchre to any of the apostles, as well as the first to see the risen Saviour. The most natural place, therefore, to assign to the vision of angels recorded by Luke (xxiv. 4-9) is that already suggested, viz., between the departure of Mary from the tomb and the arrival of Peter and John. But two questions arise here. (*a*) Is the vision of TWO ANGELS in Luke identical with the vision of ONE ANGEL in Matthew and Mark? (*b*) Are we to suppose that Mary Magdalene had already seen the angels before she went to tell Peter and John? It is strongly contended by McClellan (pp. 527-530), against the long list of commentators whom he quotes, that we are bound to infer this from the account of Matthew (xxviii. 1, 5-8) and Mark (xvi. 1, 5-8). But it seems impossible except by an extreme strain of ingenuity to reconcile this supposition with St. John's narrative. Having regard to the marvellously condensed brevity of the records, it

seems far simpler and more natural to suppose that
"the women" to whom the vision appeared were
Mary Magdalene's companions, who remained by the
tomb when she left them. Both Matthew and Mark
have referred, only a few verses previously, to "many
other women" (Matt. xxvii. 55, 56; Mark xv. 40, 41).
The angel is described by Matthew as rolling away
the stone and sitting upon it; but that he appeared
inside the sepulchre to the women (as in Mark's
account) may be inferred from his words, "*He is not
here* . . . . Come, *see the place where the Lord lay.*"
It is surely an exaggerated and fanciful precision to
lay any stress on the fact that while Mark describes
the angel as *a young man*, Luke uses a word expressing mature manhood. A mechanical coincidence in
the narratives would ill represent the excitement,
agitation, and awe of the real scene, and the tumultuous conflict of feeling with which the women "went
out quickly, and fled from the sepulchre," trembling
and bewildered, impatient to carry the astounding
news, yet speaking no word to any whom they met.
The total number of those who visited the tomb may
have been considerable; but not more than two or
three could enter the tomb at once, and probably they
were never all assembled at the same time. We may
picture them arriving along different routes by twos
and threes, as the twilight brightened into day and
the sunbeams shot up behind the mountains of Moab;
and hastily departing in various directions to carry
tidings "to the eleven and to all the rest."

(7) The narrative of St. John, taken by itself,
needs no explanation, while its inimitable beauty
almost rebukes comment. It may be useful, however, to note that the phrase "*Touch me not*" (xx.
17,—lit. "*Be not touching me;*" the *present*, not the
aorist) does not imply that Mary was forbidden at all
to touch the risen Lord, but rather that she was already
touching Him,—probably clasping His feet. The

170 OUTLINES OF THE LIFE OF CHRIST.

Lord graciously assures her that she need not seek to detain Him or fear to go on her errand, for the time of His departure, though nigh, is not yet.

Not a few judicious writers may be cited in support of the view that the appearance of our Lord to the women related in Matt. xxviii. 9, 10, simply refers, in the Evangelist's terse, generalizing manner, to the appearance to Mary Magdalene. Failing this explanation, which I confess does not seem to me satisfactory, this passage may *include* the appearance to Mary, with a separate appearance to one or more of her companions, possibly to Salome, who seems to have been the wife of Zebedee, mother of the beloved apostle, and sister to our Lord's mother.[1] The words (ver. 9), "*as they went to tell His disciples,*" are considered by most modern critics to be a gloss, not a part of the original text. The *time* of this appearance is therefore unfixed, though the supposition of Greswell (vol. iii. Diss. 6, 1st ed.) that it was not on that day, but subsequently, seems quite indefensible.

(8) The account of the appearance of our Lord in the afternoon of the day to Cleopas and a brother disciple on their way from Jerusalem to EMMAUS (about eight miles south-west of Jerusalem, *Bible Handbook*, p. 326), is given by Luke alone (xxiv. 13–35), but briefly recorded by Mark (xvi. 12, 13), whose remarkable expression, "*in another form,*" seems to imply that the means by which their eyes were holden that they should not know Him, was not simply an insensible Divine control over their perception, but also some change in our Saviour's personal appearance. This may have been partly in His apparel (a matter on which the silence of Scripture rebukes vain curiosity); but to any one who considers the marvellous change which a few hours of intense experience of joy, peril, or pain can sometimes pro-

[1] We infer this from Mark xv. 40, compared with Matt. xxvii. 56, and John xix. 25. See above, p. 120.

duce, it will seem probable that the agony of the cross, with all the suffering that preceded it, the mysterious experience of death and of the world of spirits, and the infinite joy of the victorious accomplishment of His great task, produced a transformation in our Lord's countenance, voice, and bearing, which rendered it difficult for even those who knew Him best at once to recognize Him. Yet some miraculous control over the senses of the disciples seems implied in the fact that as the Saviour blessed and broke the bread and gave it to them, "their eyes were opened, and they knew Him." His vanishing out of their sight seems parallel with John viii. 59, and perhaps Luke iv. 30.

(9) We have three accounts of the first appearance of the Saviour to THE ASSEMBLED APOSTLES: Mark xvi. 14; Luke xxiv. 36–49; John xx. 19–23. In the former two accounts they are spoken of as "the eleven," although, as the last account informs us, Thomas was absent; just as St. Paul (1 Cor. xv. 5) speaks of "the twelve," though of course perfectly aware that they had lost Judas from their number. Mark tells us that they were sitting at table, probably talking together after supper; John, that "the doors were shut for fear of the Jews;" Luke, that the two from Emmaus had arrived, and that when Jesus Himself appeared the disciples were terror-stricken, thinking they saw a spirit. This is at first sight inconsistent with what they had just before said—"*The Lord hath risen indeed, and hath appeared to Simon.*" But this is only an inconsistency such as we constantly meet with in real life. It may have chiefly arisen from the suddenness with which Jesus appeared in their midst. Luke records fully what John briefly alludes to,—the physical proof which the Saviour gave them of the reality of His risen body, by the sense of touch, by the scars in His hands, feet, and side (comp. John xx. 25, 27), and by eating

in their presence. He adds the instruction given by our Lord concerning the fulfilment of prophecy, similar to that given on the way to Emmaus, and a brief statement of the apostolic commission, more fully related by John. Mark xvi. 15–18 seems intended as a summary of our Lord's words on this and on subsequent occasions. The question of the nature of our Lord's risen body will come before us in the next section.

To sum up. We infer, not positively, but with rational probability, the following ORDER OF EVENTS.

(*a*) Soon after daybreak an angel rolls away the sealed stone; the guards swoon in terror; the Lord rises, reverently ministered to by angels (comp. John xx. 6, 7), but unseen by any human eye.

(*b*) The guards—recovering from their swoon—flee, and make their report to the priests.

(*c*) Some of the women reach the tomb before sunrise; others, including Mary Magdalene, shortly after.

(*d*) They find the tomb open and empty. Mary Magdalene (whether alone or with a companion is not clear) goes to tell Peter and John, who forthwith hasten to the spot.

(*e*) Meanwhile, to the women remaining in grief and perplexity by the sepulchre, or arriving later, an angel and afterwards two angels become visible, assuring them that the Lord is risen, and bidding them carry the glad news to their fellow-disciples. The nature of the case renders it probable, if not absolutely certain, that successive parties of women would arrive and depart at different times. The variations in the accounts are thus naturally explained. It was the object of each Evangelist to describe the main facts, not to multiply details; yet if his account was based on the reports of eye-witnesses he must describe what those witnesses actually saw and heard, though summarizing and combining their testimony.

(*f*) Peter and John, on Mary Magdalene's report, visit the tomb. The impression we gather from St. John's narrative is that they find the sepulchre deserted, and that on their departure Mary Magdalene, who has followed them, is left alone in her grief.

(*g*) Mary, looking into the sepulchre, sees the two angels, and immediately afterwards the risen Lord stands by her and talks with her. She goes to tell the Apostles and other disciples. (By this time it was probably an hour past sunrise; possibly a couple of hours, if, as some conjecture, Mary's journeys were to and from Bethany. It is likely enough that some of the disciples were at Bethany; and there is no reason to suppose that as yet the Apostles were assembled, as we find them in the evening.)

(*h*) Subsequently to the appearance to Mary Magdalene the Lord manifests Himself to one or more of her companions. (Matt. xxviii. 9, 10.)

(*i*) Some time during the day the Lord appears to Peter, first of all the Apostles. We may suppose a double reason for this: (1) to assure the penitent disciple of forgiveness; (2) to indicate that he was not to lose the leading position he had hitherto held among the Twelve, but to be the foremost preacher of the glad tidings of which the resurrection of Christ formed so vital a part.

(*j*) In the afternoon Jesus appears to two disciples journeying to Emmaus. They had left Jerusalem before any certain account had reached them that the Lord had been seen; though perhaps their words, "*But Him they saw not*," indirectly refer to a rumour that some of the women had seem Him. Even if Cleopas and his companion were aware of Mary Magdalene's report, they may have supposed that she had seen a vision. On their return to Jerusalem they find the eleven assembled, rejoicing in the fact that the Lord is risen, and has been seen by Simon. Yet their terror immediately afterwards shows them by no means yet convinced that Jesus has actually returned to bodily life. In such a case no appearance to a single witness would produce full conviction in the minds of others.

(*k*) The apostles being gathered at their evening meal, with closed doors (but Thomas absent), Jesus appears to them soon after the return of the two from Emmaus, and convinces them by touch and by eating with them that He is not a bodiless apparition but is verily risen in His crucified body from the grave. He unfolds to them the Old Testament witness to Himself, opening their understanding to receive, breathes on them in token of the bestowment of the Holy Spirit, and gives them an assurance of their apostolic authority, resembling, yet distinct from, that recorded in Matt. xvi. 19; xviii. 18.[1]

So closed that Day of Wonders, which had changed the relations of the seen and unseen world, lifted the Church from the starless gloom of despair into the morning sunshine of hope and joy; shifted the question of the life beyond the grave from the airy region of opinion, nay, even from that of mere faith, to the solid ground of experience and practical demonstration; "abolished death, ... brought life and immortality to light," and enriched us with "a living hope by THE RESURRECTION OF JESUS CHRIST FROM THE DEAD." (2 Tim. i. 10; 1 Pet. i. 3.)

A very learned and exhaustive discussion of the "particular alleged discrepancies" in the accounts of the resurrection will be found in McClellan's *Four Gospels*, pp. 508–536. Its real value may not improbably be concealed from some readers by the positive, not to say arrogant, tone with which the writer lays down his conclusions, and the contemptuous manner in which he rejects the views he

---

[1] It may be noted that the phrase (John xx. 23) "*whosesoever*," which an English reader might suppose to be in the singular, is in the Greek in the plural.

disapproves, as well as by the excessive stress laid on minor
and disputable points. But he writes as one who has
honestly looked every difficulty in the face, and has not
spared labour in getting at the truth. One point on which
Mr. McClellan (following Chrysostom) strongly insists is
that Matt. xxviii. 1 records a visit to the tomb on *Friday
evening*. But though it is true (as Lightfoot shows on
Luke xxiii. 54) that the phrase rendered "*as it began to
dawn*," might be used of the *evening* twilight, which in
Jewish reckoning was the beginning of the day; yet
Robinson (Lex., s. v. πρωί) has given proof that the preceding phrase, rendered "*in the end of the Sabbath*"—lit.,
"*late of the Sabbath*"—may correctly be translated "after
the Sabbath was past;" thus corresponding with Mark
xvi. 1. So also De Wette. Mr. McClellan has fallen into
a curious oversight on p. 532, in taking the time of sunrise
on April 9th as 5.20 a.m., which is the time in England.
In Palestine the sun rises at 5 a.m. on the longest day, and
therefore must rise at 5.20 a.m about the 21st May.

In Andrews' *Bible Student's Life of Our Lord* will be
found a careful digest of the different views of Lightfoot,
Lardner, West, Townson, Newcome, Da Costa, Greswell,
Strauss, Lange, Robinson (pp. 506-509). The writer's own
view very nearly coincides with that which I have given.
But he takes Matt. xxviii. 9, 10, to refer to the appearance
of the Lord to Mary Magdalene. On this view see Wieseler,
pp. 390-393 (Eng. Tr.); also Conder's *Lit. Hist. of New
Testament*, p. 130. The elaborate argument of Wieseler
(based on the various reading "*Joseph*" in Mark xv. 47), to
prove that "the other Mary" was the wife of Joseph of
Arimathæa, will not be likely to convince many readers.

Regarding the site of the sepulchre (of the controversy
concerning which a clear summary is also given in Mr.
Andrews' book, but of course not including the evidence
furnished by more recent exploration), the considerations
advanced by Lieut. Conder in *Tent Work* (vol. i. pp. 361-376)
appear to furnish decisive proof that the "second wall" included the spot now occupied by the "Church of the Holy
Sepulchre," which therefore cannot be the genuine site; and
further, to furnish strong evidence as to the true site of
Calvary. Mr. Fergusson's marvellous theory, that the true
site of the tomb is marked by the mosque known as the
"Dome of the Rock," of course requires no other disproof
than the establishment of the fact that this identical spot
was occupied by the "Holy of Holies;" on which point the

evidence of the rock-levels, compared with the statements of Josephus and the measurements in the Mishna, seems absolutely decisive. (See also Col. Warren's *The Temple or the Tomb*.)

SECTION III.

FROM EASTER TO PENTECOST.

SUNDAY, APRIL 9TH, TO SATURDAY, MAY 27TH (A.D. 30).

THE kingdom of God came not with observation. The change in the Divine method towards mankind, in the religious condition of the human race, and in the relation of the present life to the unseen world, wrought by the life, death, resurrection, and exaltation of Him who loved to call Himself the Son of Man, but whom the voice from heaven declared to be the Son of God, was the greatest revolution in human history. Yet no strongly marked line separated the old world from the new. The passing away of the one and the incoming of the other were like the melting of winter into spring. The Birth, the Ministry, the Death, the Resurrection, the Ascension of our Saviour, furnish each an epoch from which to reckon the new era; yet the significance of none of them was perceived until they formed one complete picture in the past, one undivided power in the thoughts and hearts of men, interpreted and applied by "the Holy Ghost sent down from heaven." (1 Peter i. 12.) Although the birth of Christ (inaccurately calculated, as it happened) is the received starting-point of the Christian Era, yet the Day of Pentecost has been justly regarded—if any single date is to be selected—as the true starting-point of the new spiritual dispensation, the birthday of the Christian

Church. And as the whole sojourn of the Son of God among men may be regarded as a border-land or isthmus between that form of God's kingdom on earth which He brought to its appointed close, and that new and more perfect form which He instituted, so the seven weeks from the Resurrection to Pentecost constitute a border-land between the work of which the Saviour said, "I have finished the work that Thou gavest Me to do," and that of which He said, "It is expedient for you that I go away; for if I go not away, the Comforter will not come unto you; but if I depart, I will send Him unto you." "As My Father hath sent Me, even so send I you." (John xvii. 4; xvi. 7; xx. 21.) It remains briefly to survey the records of this period.

The SECOND APPEARANCE of the risen Lord to His assembled apostles is recorded in the fourth Gospel only. It was on the evening of Sunday, April 16th. Thomas, "the Twin," who had been absent from the meeting that day week, was now present, and his temporary unbelief was exchanged for faith, which expressed itself in the most remarkable recorded utterance addressed to Christ by any of the disciples— "MY LORD AND MY GOD!" (John xx. 24–29.) The two verses which follow (30, 31) have been regarded as "the formal close of the Gospel," and chap. xxi. "as evidently an appendix to the Gospel, which latter was already concluded by a formal review of its contents and object" (Dean Alford). But it is very questionable whether this be more than a fancy of commentators. The connection of these two verses with our Lord's words to Thomas is so natural, and the interpolation of such a summary so much in the Evangelist's manner (comp. *e.g.* chap. ii. 23–25; xii. 37–41), that there is very slight ground for regarding them as intended to form the conclusion of his Gospel.

St. Luke tells us that Jesus "showed Himself alive after His passion" to His chosen apostles "by many infallible proofs, being seen of them forty days, and speaking of the things pertaining to the kingdom of God" (Acts i. 3). This statement suggests repeated and prolonged interviews. Three only are expressly recorded in the Gospels in addition to those already considered. An appearance to JAMES is mentioned by St. Paul only (1 Cor. xv. 7). It seems probable, since no reason can be imagined for a distinct appearance to any of the apostles (Peter's case standing alone), that the James here named was neither the son of Zebedee nor the son of Alphæus, but "James the Lord's brother" (Gal. i. 19). Accepting the view that he was one of the unbelieving brethren referred to in John vii. 3-5, 10, that these were sons of Joseph and Mary, and that this was the James afterwards famous as "THE JUST," president of the mother Church at Jerusalem, we may well imagine the importance of this appearance of the risen Lord, and are naturally led to connect it with the presence of "His brethren" with the assembled believers at Jerusalem. (Acts i. 14.)

The THREE REMAINING APPEARANCES recorded in the Gospels are (A), one to seven of the apostles by the Lake of Galilee (John xxi. 1-22); (B), to an assembly of disciples, solemnly appointed, in a mountain in Galilee (Matt. xxviii. 16-20); and (C), the final meeting with the disciples at Jerusalem and Bethany (Luke xxiv. 49-51; Acts i. 4-12). The appearance to James was between the second and third of these (1 Cor. xv. 6, 7)—probably in Galilee.

(A) The return of the disciples from Jerusalem to Galilee was not simply a return to their homes after the Passover, but an act of obedience to the express command of Christ. (See Matt. xxvi. 32; xxviii. 7, 16.) Since the intercourse of the disciples with their risen Lord was not continuous and familiar as of old, but occasional, there was nothing blameworthy, but the reverse, in the proposal of the ever-active Simon that in the interval of unemployed time they should betake themselves to their old occupation on the Lake. The five who are named as being present on this occasion were apostles, and it seems a natural inference that the two unnamed were apostles likewise. All night they toiled, and as once before, three years ago, they took nothing. The unlooked-for visit of the Lord Jesus, as the morning twilight brightened into day, taught, not for them only, but for us, the blessed lesson that His presence may be looked for in the midst of common scenes and honest toil no less than in Church gatherings or solitary prayer. The miraculous draught, the unbroken net, and the meal provided on the shore, were symbols full of cheer, of the success of their ministry, and of their Lord's power to provide for their need. The lessons of this closing scene of St. John's Gospel are treated with great beauty as well as learning—perhaps with exuberance of mystical fancy—by Archbishop Trench (*On Miracles*, pp. 462-485). He seems to go beyond the record, and even to contradict our Saviour's words, "*Bring of the fish which ye have now caught,*" when he says, "'The character of the meal was sacramental, and it had nothing to do with the stilling of their present hunger."

If the thrice-repeated question to Peter, with evident allusion to his thrice-repeated denial, humbled him before the eyes of his brethren, the thrice-repeated charge to act as under-shepherd of Christ's flock honoured him as being fully restored to his office and work. (Comp. 1 Peter v. 1–4.) The statement in John xxi. 23 is deeply interesting, as showing the possibility of the early currency of a false tradition even among the apostles; and thus strongly illustrating the indispensable necessity of the promised guidance of "the Spirit of truth" (chap. xvi. 13).

This seems the fitting place to refer to an opinion to which great importance has been attached, and which is thus stated by Archbishop Trench, who quotes

180 OUTLINES OF THE LIFE OF CHRIST.

Ambrose and Chrysostom to the same effect: "Doubtless there is a significance in the words '*showed Himself*' or '*manifested Himself*,' which many long ago observed,—no other than this—that His body after the resurrection was only visible by a distinct act of His will. From that time the disciples did not as before see Jesus, but Jesus *appeared unto them*, or *was seen by them*" (page 463). Dean Alford and Dr. Westcott may be cited as entertaining similar views. The latter speaks of our Lord's risen body as "glorified." "The body which was recognized as essentially the same body had yet undergone some marvellous change, of which we gain a faint idea by what is directly recorded of its manifestations. Under a physical image, that change is presented to us by our Lord Himself in the absence of blood, the symbol and seat of corruptible life. Luke xxiv. 39; Eph. v. 30" (*The Gospel of the Resurrection*, p. 139). In these two passages, our Saviour's body is spoken of as having "flesh and bones," not flesh and blood. Hence Dr. Westcott infers that it was *bloodless*, the whole of the blood having been shed on the cross. But a body of bloodless flesh and bone would no more be a "glorified body" than a body of flesh and blood; it would be a corpse, with no heart beating in its bosom, breathing no breath of life; a ghastly apparition, which might well have filled the Apostles with more terror than if they had "seen a spirit." When the Lord bade them "handle" Him, to see that it was His very self, and showed the scars in His hands and feet and side, did the eager touch (to which St. John alludes in his First Epistle, i. 1) rest on the marble rigidity of a bloodless corpse, or on warm living flesh? Did our Saviour when He ate and drank in their presence mean to cheat them into a false belief, or was not their belief as true as it was natural, that His risen body was the same, and of the same nature, as the body which suffered on the cross?

It is urged that our Saviour's body, after His resurrection, could not have been subject to ordinary laws, since He vanished at will and entered a room with closed doors. This argument proves too much, since a real body of *flesh and bone* could no more vanish, or pass through a door, without a miracle, than a body of *flesh and blood*. As to the first, the parallel instances in John viii. 59; x. 39; Luke iv. 30, have already been referred to. As to the second, it may be that the door opened of "its own accord," like that of Peter's prison (Acts xii. 10); but if not, the miracle is not a greater reversal of ordinary phenomena than that of walking on the water. It seems to furnish a special stumbling-block to minds which mistake our total ignorance of the inmost constitution of matter for knowledge. But if there be anything more than an antiquated assumption in "the impenetrability of matter," about which so much has been said, it pertains only to the invisible atoms; and to One possessing perfect knowledge and unbounded control of all material objects, it would be probably as easy to pass bodily through an oaken plank or a sheet of metal as for us it would be easy to pass a hot knife through a bar of wax. If we believe in the reality of the Gospel miracles, it is inconsistent and fanciful to find a difficulty in one physical miracle more than another.

We conclude, therefore, that during the six weeks from His Resurrection to His Ascension, although for wise but unknown reasons the Scripture is silent regarding the greater part of that interval, the Lord Jesus breathed and moved as a living man among men; and that not until He quitted this earth did His body undergo that glorious change of which the Transfiguration was a silent prophecy, and which shall pass on the bodies of all His saints, when He "shall transform our body of humiliation into the likeness of His body of glory, according to the energy of His power, even to subdue all things unto Himself." (Phil. iii. 21; comp. 1 Cor. xv. 35-38, 44, 49-53.)

(B) The appearance to the assembled disciples in a MOUNTAIN IN GALILEE, recorded by St. Matthew, is commonly supposed to be the same with the appearance to "more than five hundred brethren at once," referred to by St. Paul. This identification has been called in question, but no reason has been shown for doubting it. It is incredible that our Lord would have convened a meeting of five hundred disciples in Jerusalem; and if in Galilee it could hardly be other than that recorded by St. Matthew. The repeated references to the meeting beforehand, and the stress laid on its express appointment, show that it was an occasion of great importance. The angel's words, "He goeth before YOU into Galilee; there shall YE see Him," imply that others as well as the Eleven were to be present. Our Lord's most numerous and devoted disciples were in Galilee; and the benefit and even necessity of holding at least one general gathering are obvious, both for the furtherance of their faith and joy, and for the confirmation of the apostolic witness. St. Matthew's remark that "some doubted" seems plainly to refer not to the Eleven, but to others assembled with them; and he leaves us to infer that these doubts vanished when "Jesus came and spake unto them." What is often spoken of as "THE APOSTOLIC· COMMISSION" was therefore delivered, not to the Eleven alone, but to the whole Christian Church as there represented. So we find it afterwards understood and acted on, when, while the Apostles remained in Jerusalem, "they that were scattered abroad went everywhere preaching the word." Mark xvi. 15-18 may probably be regarded as a concise reference to the same great occasion.

(C) It is a striking example of the marvellously condensed brevity of the Gospel narratives, to which modern critics are fond of applying the term "fragmentary," that while the Fourth Gospel confirms the First as to the fact that the disciples returned to Galilee, and that the Lord there manifested Himself to them, the Second and Third Gospels give no hint of their quitting Jerusalem; and but for the fuller account in Acts we might understand St. Luke to narrate the Ascension as having taken place on the evening of the same day as the Resurrection. To suppose that this and similar silent omissions, which everywhere characterize the Gospel, indicate "imperfect information," or are correctly characterized as "fragmentary," is, I believe, to misconceive the character and purpose of the Gospels. It is like charging the painter of a set of historical pictures with ignorance of all the events he has not painted, and censuring him for avoiding cross-lights and overcrowding of his canvas.

The fact that Bethany is mentioned as the spot from which our Lord ascended suggests the conjecture—it can be nothing more—that others of the disciples besides the Eleven witnessed that glorious farewell; Lazarus, perhaps, and his sisters, and possibly the mother and brethren of Jesus.

There is no reason to suppose that "the cloud" which "received Him out of their sight" was like the "bright cloud" on the Mount of Transfiguration; rather, it was a majestic veil, screening this great event from common eyes, and checking the too curious gaze of the disciples themselves. As they vainly tried to penetrate the veil, unable to believe the reality of what their eyes had witnessed, two angels from the legions which (we cannot doubt) attended the Lord on His homeward way, bade them connect in their faith and hope this wondrous parting with the literal personal return in the appointed season of the glorified Jesus.

" So then after the Lord had spoken unto them, HE WAS RECEIVED UP INTO HEAVEN, AND SAT ON THE RIGHT HAND OF GOD." (Mark xvi. 19.)

The "FORTY DAYS" mentioned by St. Luke, reckoned from Sunday, April 9th *inclusively*, give Thursday, May 18th, as the day of the Ascension. Nine days—or ten *inclusive*—remained to Pentecost. Pentecost was the Greek name of the "Feast of Weeks," "Feast of Harvest," or "Day of First-fruits." (Ex. xxxiv. 22; xxiii. 16; Num. xxviii. 26.) This was the sixth of the month Sivan, seven full weeks, or fifty days *inclusive*, from the day on which the sheaf was offered in the Temple. It consequently always fell on the same week-day with the second day of Passover (Nisan 16). The hypothesis which places the Crucifixion on the 14th Nisan therefore makes the Day of Pentecost fall on a Sunday; but since, as we have seen, the day of the Crucifixion was in reality Friday, Nisan 15, Nisan 16 was Sabbath, and Pentecost consequently fell on a Sabbath, viz. Saturday, May 27th. Since this Feast was the anniversary of the giving of the law on Mount Sinai, there was a special and solemn appropriateness in its being chosen as the public starting-point of the new dispensation; the first proclamation to Israel and to the world of that Gospel which bids us come not "to the mount that could be touched and that burned with fire," but "unto Mount Sion, and unto the city of the living God, the heavenly Jerusalem, and to Jesus, the Mediator of the New Covenant." (Heb. xii. 18–24.)

The rapture of Elijah to heaven has been compared to the soaring of a bird which none can follow; the ascension of Jesus, to the building of a bridge between earth and heaven. As the DEATH of Christ, revealing God's love in His justice, and God's justice in His love, changed the moral relation of mankind to the law of God (Rom. iii. 25, 26; v. 8; 2 Cor. v. 19–21; 1 John i. 9), and the RESURRECTION of Christ, bringing the life beyond death within the circle of facts proved by experience, changed the intellectual relation of the life here to the life hereafter (1 Cor. xv. 20; 2 Tim. i. 10;

1 Peter i. 3), so the ASCENSION of Christ has changed the relation of the seen to the unseen world in regard to emotion and affection, hope and love; rendering it for the first time possible to fix the supreme warmth and purest passion of human affection and to concentrate the steady purpose of daily life upon the unseen Saviour and the home above. (John xiv. 1–4; xvii. 24; Col. iii. 1–4; 1 Peter, i. 7, 8; 1 John iii. 3.) The DAY OF PENTECOST in like manner revolutionized the relation of the Church to the World. It substituted as the ground of religious fellowship in place of the outward unity of national descent, rites, and laws, the spiritual unity of personal faith in Christ, knowledge of His truth, obedience to His commands, love to His disciples, and the possession of His Spirit. (John xv. 9, 10, 12; xvii. 20–23; Acts ii. 41–47; Eph. iv. 4–13; Heb. viii. 6, 10–13; xii. 18–24.)

The ten days which intervened between the parting on Mount Olivet and the outpouring of the Holy Spirit were spent by the assembled disciples in earnest united prayer. (Acts i. 13, 14.) We may perhaps be permitted to conjecture that this interval was occupied in the triumphal progress of the glorified Redeemer to that central scene of His sovereignty, figuratively spoken of as "the right hand of God." On that day He began to fulfil His promise, "If I depart I will send Him unto you;" and in so doing, His earlier promise, "On this rock I will build My Church."

The GOSPEL HISTORY, therefore, is not to be regarded as closing even the Day of Pentecost. The book which Church tradition has not very accurately named "The Acts of the Apostles," is in very deed the second book of Luke's Gospel. As the first treats in brief outline of "all things that Jesus began both to do and to teach until the day in which He was taken up," so this contains the story of all that He proceeded "to do and to teach," through the ministry of His servants, "being by the right hand of God exalted, and having received of the Father the promise of the Holy Ghost." As a rule (with exceptions, as chap. iv. 24, 26, 29), when "the Lord" is spoken of in this book, the Lord Jesus personally is intended. In the first twelve chapters, viii. 1-13, 26-40; ix. 1-30 excepted, He is seen carrying on the work of building His Church by the ministry of that Apostle to whom He had promised the keys; whose it was to open the Kingdom first (chap. ii.) to Israel, and then (chap. x.) to the Gentiles. In chap. ix. the Lord is seen personally calling the future Apostle of the Gentiles; and from chap. xiii. onwards the extension of the Kingdom by the multiplication of Christian Churches, during more than thirty years from the Ascension, is exhibited as wrought principally, though by no means exclusively, by that greatest of Christian teachers; until in the Metropolis of the world we see "Paul the prisoner of Christ" in chains, yet "preaching the Kingdom of God, and teaching those things which concern the Lord Jesus Christ, with all confidence, UNHINDERED."

INDEX OF TEXTS.

MATTHEW.

CH. AND VER.	PAGE	CH. AND VER.	PAGE	CH. AND VER.	PAGE
i.	30, 31	x. 2-4	82	xviii.	109
ii.	34, 35	,, 1-42	96, 97	xix. 1-12	111, 112
,, 23	37	xi. 1	ib.	,, 13-30	116
iii. 1-12	5-49	,, 2-19	86	xx. 1-16	ib.
,, 13-17	49, 50	,, 12-14	67	,, 17-28	119, 120
iv. 1-11	ib.	,, 20-30	87	,, 29-34	120, 121
,, 12-17	67	,, 28-30	56	xxi. 1-17	121, 122
,, 12	61, 64	xii. 1-8	81	,, 12	124
,, 13	69	,, 9-14	ib.	,, 18-46	124, 125
,, 17	60, 66	,, 15-21	82	xxii. 1-14	125
,, 18-22	68	,, 22-50	88	,, 15-46	126
,, 23-25	60	xiii. 1	84	xxiii. 1	57
v.-vii.	72	,, 1-52	90	,, 1-39	126
vii. 28	71	,, 53-58	65, 95	xxiv. 1-51	127
viii. 2	56	xiv. 1-13	98	xxv. 1-46	ib.
,, 2-4	72	,, 14-34	99	xxvi. 1-5	128, 130
,, 5	69	,, 33	56	,, 6-16	123
,, 5-13	84	,, 34-36	100	,, 17-35	130, 140
,, 14-17	69	,, 35	101	,, 36-46	141
,, 18-27	91	xv. 1-28	104	,, 47-56	ib.
,, 28-34	92	,, 24	57	,, 57-75	141, 146
ix. 1-28	ib.	,, 25	56	xxvii. 1-10	146, 147
,, 2-9	73	,, 29-39	105, 106	,, 11-25	149-152
,, 10-17	74, 93	xvi. 5-12	106	,, 26	151
,, 18	56	,, 21-28	107	,, 27-56	153-159
,, 18-26	93	,, 22	103	,, 57-66	161, 162
,, 27-34	94	xvii. 1-21	108	xxviii. 1-15	163-174
,, 35	70	,, 22-27	109	,, 16-20	178, 182
,, 35-38	95, 96	,, 24	70		

MARK.

CH. AND VER.	PAGE	CH. AND VER.	PAGE	CH. AND VER.	PAGE
i. 1-4	45	v. 1-21	92	ix. 30-50	109
,, 5-8	47, 48	,, 6	56	x. 1-12	111
,, 9-11	48	,, 21	74	,, 13-31	116
,, 12, 13	48, 49	,, 22-43	93	,, 32-45	119, 120
,, 14	60, 61, 67	vi. 1	94	,, 46	120, 121
,, 15	67	,, 1-6	65	xi. 1-11	121, 122
,, 16-20	68	,, 3	42	,, 12-19	125
,, 21-28	69, 70	,, 7-13	96	,, 20-26	ib.
,, 35-39	70	,, 14-29	98	,, 27-33	ib.
,, 40-45	72	,, 20	56	xii. 1-12	ib.
ii. 1-12	73	,, 30-53	99	,, 13-44	126
,, 6	74	,, 39	98	xiii. 1-37	127
,, 14	73	,, 54-56	100	xiv. 1-2	128, 130
,, 15-32	74, 93	,, 55	101	,, 3-11	130
,, 23-28	81	vii. 1-23	104	,, 12-31	130-140
iii. 1-6	ib.	,, 14	57	,, 32-42	141
,, 7-19	82	,, 24-30	104	,, 43-52	ib.
,, 19	84	,, 31-37	105	,, 53-72	142-147
,, 21	83	viii. 1-10	106	xv. 1-21	147-154
,, 22-35	88	,, 19	ib.	,, 25	154-159
,, 31	42	,, 22-30	106, 107	,, 22-41	156-159
iv. 1-35	90	,, 31-38	107	,, 42-47	161
,, 35	84	ix. 1	ib.	xvi. 1-18	163-174
,, 35-41	91	,, 2-29	108	,, 19, 20	183

LUKE.

CH. AND VER.	PAGE	CH. AND VER.	PAGE	CH. AND VER.	PAGE
i., ii.	30-33	iv. 42-44	70, 71	viii. 22-25	91
ii. 1-3	18, 19	v. 1-11	60, 71	,, 26-39	92
,, 4-20	11-21	,, 11	68	,, 40	74
,, 40	34	,, 12-26	72	,, 41-56	93
,, 41-52	39	,, 27-39	73, 93	ix. 1-6	96
iii. 1, 2	45	vi. 1	77	,, 7	57
,, 3-18	47	,, 1-5	81	,, 10	98
,, 19, 20	61	,, 6-11	ib.	,, 11-17	99
,, 21-23	49	,, 12-19	82	,, 18-27	107
,, 23	45	,, 20-49	72, 82	,, 28-45	108
iv. 1-13	49, 50	vii. 1-10	84	,, 46-50	109
,, 14	60, 64	,, 11-17	85	,, 51-56	111-115
,, 14, 15	67	,, 18-35	86	,, 57-62	115
,, 16-30	65	,, 36-50	87	x. 1-20	112-115
,, 30	55	,, 37	56	,, 13-15	87
,, 31	69	viii. 1-3	88	,, 21-24	ib.
,, 31-37	70	,, 4-18	90	,, 25-42	115
,, 38-41	ib.	,, 19-21	88	xi. 1-13	97

INDEX OF TEXTS.

CH. AND VER.	PAGE	CH. AND VER.	PAGE	CH. AND VER.	PAGE
xi. 14–26	88	xviii. 1–30	115	xxii. 17–39	130–140
,, 29–36	97	,, 31–34	119	,, 40–46	141
,, 37–54	ib.	,, 35–43	120, 121	,, 47–65	141-146
xii. 1–59	ib.	xix. 1–28	121	,, 66–71	147
xiii. 1–9, 31, 32	103, 104	,, 29–44	121–123	xxiii.	ib.
,, 10–21	104	,, 45, 46	124	,, 2–26	149–154
,, 22–35	115	,, 47, 48	125, 126	,, 27–32	156
xiv. 1–24	ib.	xx.	126	,, 33–49	157, 158
,, 25–35	ib.	xxi. 1–4	ib.	,, 50–56	161
xv.	ib.	,, 5–36	127	xxiv. 1–49	164–174
xvi.	ib.	,, 37, 38	ib.	,, 36–43	180, 181
xvii.	ib.	xxii. 1–6	130	,, 50–53	183, 184
		,, 7–16	130, 131		

JOHN.

i. 6–28	46–48	vii. 2–53	109, 110	xii. 20-50	126
,, 29–51	48–51	,, 5	42	xiii.–xvii.	130–139
,, 1–12	51, 52	,, 40–46	71	xviii. 1–12	140
,, 13–17	52, 53	viii. 1–11	110	,, 6	55
,, 18–22	45	,, 12	111	,, 13–27	141–146
,, 23–25	58	,, 12–59	117	,, 28	147
iii.	58–61	ix., x.	117	,, 29–32	149
iv. 1–3	59–63	ix. 38	56	,, 33–40	149–151
,, 35	58	x. 22	110, 116	xix. 1–18	151–153
,, 4–54	65	,, 40	111	,, 14	154, 155
v. 1	77	xi. 1–54	118	,, 19–37	156–159
,, 1–47	78–80	,, 8	103	,, 38–42	161
vi. 1	81	,, 47–50	57	,, 31	162
,, 1–12	99	,, 55	77	xx. 1–23	163–174
,, 4	77, 98	xii. 1–11	123	,, 24–31	177
,, 22–71	100	,, 12–19	121	xxi.	178–181
vii. 1	101				

LONDON:
PRINTED BY WILLIAM CLOWES AND SONS, LIMITED,
STAMFORD STREET AND CHARING CROSS.

www.ingramcontent.com/pod-product-compliance
Lightning Source LLC
Chambersburg PA
CBHW032146160426
43197CB00008B/784